Baseball's Greatest Players

By Frank Mackay and Gordon Mackay

ISBN 13: 978-1-942500-18-6

ISBN 10: 1-942500-18-6

Forward

This book is the compilation of decades of research by our Father Joseph MacKay. From our earliest memories in the early 70's he would spend countless hours each week researching Baseball Statistics.

Please remember, this was the 1970's and the Internet, Google etc. wasn't even a glimmer in anyone's eye. Therefore research on the statistics of the game was a laborious process but a passion for the man. He would search libraries throughout the New York Tri-State area and Cooperstown itself. Searching old newspapers and microfilms for stats from the 20th and even the 19th centuries.

In many ways our Dad was a pioneer of how research, facts and statistics was another way and in many cases a more accurate way to document the history of baseball. In recent decades Sabermetrics has been growing much more of an acceptable thing.

Bill James who gained prominence in the 1980's is probably the most famous and successful of Baseball Researchers. In 2003 James was hired by Red Sox owner John Henry as a Senior Advisor of Baseball Operations. He has even earned three World Series Rings 2004, 2007 & 2013.

Sandy Alderson GM of the New York Mets started utilizing the principals of Sabermetrics in the earl 1990's. As GM of the Oakland A's, Alderson used these principles as a method in obtaining under-valued players.

Billy Beane GM of the Oakland A's who was immortalized in the film Moneyball; while he's not a public proponent of Sabermetrics, has used its principles since the late 1990's in keeping his low budget team in contention.

Paul DePodesta joined the Oakland A's in 1999 as an assistant to GM Billy Beane. He was featured in the book and film Moneyball. DePodesta moved done the coast in 2004 to become GM of the Dodgers. He has worked as a front office advisor for the Padres and the Mets. He has recently been hired by the NFL's Cleveland Browns as Chief Strategy Officer.

With so many Sports Franchises now using Stats to run their teams, it proves that Joe MacKay was a true visionary.

Legal pad after legal pad would be filled with scribbled notes, stats and facts that for decades was his release from the real world. After his passing we found boxes filled with this research. It was decided by us that our Father's life and research wouldn't be complete without it being shared. That is why we hope you enjoy the following, and for many a look at the game of baseball through the numbers and facts.

- Frank and Gordon MacKay, May 2016

Two or More ERA Leaders for the Same Team while Teammates

This has happened several times since ERA statistics have been kept. Officially, ERA averages kept by the leagues started in 1912 with the National League. The following year the American League followed suit.

Starting in 1969, when devoted baseball purists wanted to create a more precise and accurate record book, baseball stats became more expanded. Earned run averages were calculated all the way back to 1876.

Examining the earned run average leaders during the modern baseball ERA (1900 on), there have been thirty-three times teammates pitching for the same team were leaders in that department.

Surprisingly, only five times were there more than two teammates who were ERA leaders. The one time it happened in the American League was in 1916, when the Boston Red Sox had three. The glitch here is when the 1916 winner Babe Ruth followed Joe Wood, the 1915 winner. In 1916, Wood did not pitch that year due to his being a holdout. Wood still belonged to the Boston Red Sox and could have played if desired.

In the National League, the Cincinnati Reds in 1944 became the first to have more than two ERA leaders. The New York Giants matched this in the years 1952 and 1953. When the Giants moved to San Francisco they had four ERA leaders on the same staff.

ERA Teammates

American League

Cleveland	1903	Chicago	1907-1913
E. Moore	1903	D. White	1906
A. Joss	1904	E. Walsh	1907 & 1910

National League

New York	1905-1908	Chicago	1907-1911
McGinnity	1904	M. Brown	1906
Mathewson	1905	J. Pfiester	1907

Teammates Who Were ERA Leaders Two or More Times

American League

Boston 1914-1916		Washington	1925
D. Leonard	1914	W. Johnson	1924
J. Wood	1915	S. Coveleski	1925
B. Ruth	1916		

Chicago	1942
T. Lee	1941
T. Lyons	1942

*In 1916, Wood did not pitch due to being a holdout. He was still Boston property.

Detroit	1945-1946	New York	1953
D. Trout	1944	A. Reynolds	1952
H. Newhouser	1945 & 1946	E. Lopat	1953

New York	1958	Chicago	1963
W. Ford	1956 & 1957	F. Bauman	1960
B. Shantz	1957	G. Peters	1963

Chicago	1967	Cleveland	1968
G. Peters	1963 & 1966	S. McDowell	1965
J. Horlen	1967	L. Tiant	1968

Oakland	1971	Oakland	1974
D. Segui	1970	V. Blue	1971
V. Blue	1971	C. Hunter	1974

New York	1980	Baltimore	1984
R. Guidry	1978 & 1979	J. Palmer	1973
R. May	1980	J. Palmer	1975
		M. Boddicker	1984

Toronto	1987	Toronto	1998
D. Stieb	1985	J. Guzman	1996
J. Key	1987	R. Clemens	1997 & 1998

National League

New York	1913	Chicago	1919-1920
J. Tesreau	1912	H. Vaughn	1918
C. Mathewson	1913	G. Alexander	1919 & 1920

St. Louis	1943	Cincinnati	1944
M. Cooper	1942	B. Walters	1939 & 1940
H. Pollet	1943	E. Riddle	1941
		E. Heusser	1944

St. Louis	1948-1951	Boston	1951
H. Pollet	1943 & 1946	W. Spahn	1947
H. Brecheen	1948	C. Nichols	1951

New York	1952	New York	1954
D. Koslo	1949	J. Hearn	1950
J. Hearn	1950	H. Wilhelm	1952
H. Wilhelm	1952	J. Antonelli	1954

Milwaukee	1956-1963	San Francisco	1960
W. Spahn	1947, 1953 & 1961	J. Antonelli	1954
L. Burdette	1956	S. Miller	1958
		S. Jones	1959
		M. McCormick	1960

Atlanta	1974	Houston	1981-1982
P. Niekro	1967	D. Sutton	1980
B. Capra	1974	N. Ryan	1981
Houston	1980-1988	Houston	1990
N. Ryan	1981 & 1987	M. Scott	1986
M. Scott	1986	D. Darwin	1990

Pitchers That Have One Hundred Wins in Both Leagues.

In 2003, Randy Johnson joined the list of pitchers who achieved one hundred wins in both leagues. His six wins in 2003 gave him exactly one hundred National League victories. Five of the seven have been enshrined in Cooperstown, with Randy paving the way for his eventual entrance. Looking at this list Cy Young stands out as the only pitcher to gather two hundred wins in both leagues.

Just a note that Milt Pappas failed to make this list due to his only having 99 National League wins.

Name	American League	National League
J. Bunning	118	106
F. Jenkins	115	169
R. Johnson	130	100
D. Martinez	141	104
G. Perry	139	175
N. Ryan	189	135
C. Young	222	289

Twenty Wins and Twenty Losses in the Same Year Since 1900

Before the turn of the twentieth century, pitchers with twenty plus wins and twenty plus losses were fairly common. The reason for this was in the early years, there were only one and two man pitching staffs. Also, pitchers finished what they started as there were no relief specialists. When teams started to employ the four man rotations, the chance for twenty to twenty men diminished. Since modern baseball (1900 on), there have been only eleven twenty to twenty men. Before 1900, in the National League twenty to twenty men occurred seventy-six times. It happened forty-four times in the American Association. The Union Association, in its one existence, had three twenty to twenty twirlers. The players had four in its one-year life.

Of the eleven pitchers of the twentieth century, only two men did it twice. Joe McGinnity did it in the American League's initial seasonal and in the National League in 1903, posting thirty-one wins. He is the only one to do it in both leagues.

George Mullin also did twenty to twenty twice both times that he was a .500 pitcher. Mullin is the only one to pitch for a pennant winner. He helped the Detroit Tigers clinch their maiden championship. Mullin did have two twenty-five game pitcher to compensate for his breakeven record.

American League

J. McGinnity	1901	Baltimore	26-20
B. Dinneen	1902	Boston	21-21
G. Mullin	1905	Detroit	21-21
G. Mullin	1907	Detroit	20-20
J. Scott	1913	Chicago	20-20
W. Johnson	1916	Washington	25-20
W. Wood	1973	Chicago	24-20

National League

V. Willis	1902	Boston	27-20
J. McGinnity	1903	New York	31-20
I. Young	1905	Boston	20-21
P. Niekro	1979	Atlanta	21-20

Three Teammates with No-Hitter on the Same Staff

There have been several occasions that teams have had two pitchers on the same staff with no-hitters. Teams that have had three on the same staff is a rarity. Only four teams had. The last time it was done was when Bob Lemon, in 1948, tossed a two to zero no-hitter for the Cleveland Indians. He joined teammates Bob Feller and Don Black on the staff. The oddity was that all three threw them in consecutive years, from 1946 to 1948. Listed below are the teams with the pitchers and year they threw their gems.

Boston American League   1905
C. Young   1904
J. Tannehill   1904
B. Dinneen   1905

New York   National League   1912
C. Mathewson   1901 & 1905
H. Wiltse   1908
J. Tesreau   1912

New York   National League   1915
C. Mathewson   1901 & 1905
J. Tesreau   1912
R. Marquard   1915

Cleveland   American League   1948
B. Feller   1940 & 1946
D. Black   1947
B. Lemon   1948

* Note that in 1915, Marquard pitched his no-hitter against Brooklyn. Later that year he was traded to Brooklyn.

Three or More Teammates No-Hitter Same Staff

American League	1948	Cleveland	B. Feller	1940 & 1946
			D. Black	1947
			B. Lemon	1948

Black suffered cerebral hemorrhage injury during the season

National League	1915	New York	C. Mathewson	1901 & 1905
			J. Tesreau	1912
			R. Marquard	1915
	1912	New York	C. Mathewson	1901 & 1905
			H. Wiltse	1908
			J. Tesreau	1912
	1905	Boston	C. Young	1904
			J. Tannehill	1904
			B. Dinneen	1905

Twenty Game Winners in Both Leagues

During the early part of the twentieth century, the newly formed American and the older National League engaged in raiding each other's ball players. This enabled many pitchers to gain twenty game seasons in both leagues. After the bidding war between the leagues ended, team rosters stabilized with player movement done through trades. This was only done within the league. *A total of eleven pitchers in the first decade and the beginning of interleague trading in the 1960's, and free agency in 1970's, only one pitcher could claim the distinction of winning twenty in both leagues.* That was Carl Mays who was waived from the American League to the National League.

From the 1960's, and after nine other pitchers claimed twenty win seasons in both leagues. Listed are those pitchers.

C. Young	American League:	Boston:	1901-1904, 1907 & 1908
	National League:	Cleveland:	1891-1898,
		St. Louis:	1899-1900
A. Orth	American League:	New York:	1906
	National League:	Philadelphia:	1901
B. Donovan	American League:	Detroit:	1907
	National League:	Brooklyn:	1901
J. McGinnity	American League:	Baltimore:	1901
	National League:	Brooklyn:	1899-1900
		New York:	1903-1906
C. Mays	American League:	Boston:	1917-1918
		New York:	1920-1921
	National League:	Cincinnati:	1924
C. Griffith	American League:	Chicago:	1901
	National League:	Chicago:	1897-1899
C. Fraser	American League:	Philadelphia:	1901
	National League:	Philadelphia:	1899
G. Perry	American League:	Cleveland:	1972 & 1974
		San Diego:	19
	National League:	San Francisco:	1966 & 1970
J. Powell	American League:	St. Louis:	1902
		New York:	1904
	National League:	Cleveland:	1898

		St. Louis:	1899
B. Singer	American League:	California:	1973
	National League:	Los Angles:	1969
F. Jenkins	American League:	Texas:	1974
	National League:	Chicago:	1967-1972
F. Donahue	American League:	St. Louis:	1902
	National League:	Philadelphia:	1899 & 1901
A. Messersmith	American League:	California:	1971
	National League:	Los Angeles:	1974
J. Chesbro	American League:	New York	1903, 1904 & 1906
	National League:	Pittsburgh:	1901-1902
J. Koosman	American League:	Minnesota:	1979
	National League:	New York:	1976
J. Tannehill	American League:	Boston:	1904-1905
	National League:	Pittsburgh:	1898-1900 & 1902
T. John	American League:	New York	1979-1980
	National League:	Los Angeles:	1977
B. Dinneen	American League:	Boston:	1902-1904
	National League:	Boston:	1900
F. Viola	American League:	Minnesota:	1988
	National League:	New York:	1990

D. Cone	American League:	New York:	1998
	National League:	New York:	1990
R. Johnson	American League:	Seattle:	1997
	National League:	Arizona:	2001-2002

Teams with a Twenty Game Winner in the Same Year.

This rarity of events occurred four times in baseball history. The first time it happened was in 1881, when the pitching distance was forty-five feet. All eight teams boasted a twenty game winner.

The next time that a twenty game winner emerged on every team's staff was in the American Association during the 1886 campaign. Eleven pitchers joined the charmed circle that would be the first time at the fifty-foot distance. During 1891, twelve pitchers in the National League copped twenty or more wins, with early staff having at least one.

In 1892, the game saw the demise of the American Association. The National League expanded to twelve teams by adding four of the Defunct Association's teams. Unbelievably, all twelve entries sprouted a twenty game winner. There were twenty-two who gathered in twenty or more victories. That would be a major league record.

National League 1881

Team Finish	Pitcher	Team	Record
1	Larry Corcoran	Chicago	31-14
2	H. Radbourn	Providence	25-11
3	P. Galvin	Buffalo	29-24
4	G. Derby	Detroit	29-26
5	M. Welch	Troy	21-18
6	J. Whitney	Boston	31-33
7	J. McCormick	Cleveland	26-30
8	L. Richmond	Worcester	25-27

13

Note: Chicago had two twenty game winners in 1881.

American Association 1886

Team Finish	Pitcher	Team	Record
1	D. Foutz	St. Louis	41-16
2	E. Morris	Pittsburgh	41-20
3	H. Porter	Brooklyn	28-20
4	G. Hecker	Louisiana	27-23
5	T.Mullane	Cincinnati	31-27
6	A. Atkinson	Philadelphia	25-17
7	J. Lynch	New York	20-20
8	M. Kilroy	Baltimore	29-34

Note: St. Louis had two twenty game winners in 1886
Cincinnati had two twenty game winners in 1886
Pittsburgh had two twenty game winners in 1886

National League 1891

Team Finish	Pitcher	Team	Record
1	J. Clarkson	Boston	33-19
2	B. Hutchinson	Chicago	43-19
3	A. Rusie	New York	32-19
4	K. Gleason	Philadelphia	24-19
5	C. Young	Cleveland	27-20
6	T. Lovett	Brooklyn	21-20
7	T. Mullane	Cincinnati	24-25
8	M. Baldwin	Pittsburgh	21-27

Note: Boston had three twenty game winners in 1891
New York had two twenty game winners in 1891
Philadelphia had two twenty game winners in 1891

National League 1892

Team Finish	Pitcher	Team	Record
1	K. Nichols	Boston	35-16

2	C. Young	Cleveland	36-11
3	G. Haddock	Brooklyn	31-13
4	G. Weyhing	Philadelphia	28-18
5	T. Mullane	Cincinnati	21-10
6	M. Baldwin	Pittsburgh	27-20
7	B. Hutchinson	Chicago	37-34
8	A. Rusie	New York	31-28
9	S. Stratton	Louisville	21-19
10	F. Killen	Washington	30-23
11	K. Gleason	St. Louis	20-24
12	J. McMahon	Baltimore	20-25

Note: Boston had three twenty game winners in 1892
Cleveland had two twenty game winners in 1892
Chicago had two twenty game winners in 1892
Brooklyn had two twenty game winners in 1892

Pitchers with Two or More No-Hitters.

When Cy Young pitched his perfect game in 1904, he did something for the first time. He became the first man to pitch a no-hitter in two different centuries. His perfect complemented his first no-hitter, which was twirled in 1897.

The dawn of the 21st century gave Hideo Nomo the distinction of pitching the initial no-hit, no run game in the new century. This also made him the second pitcher to spin a no-hitter in two different centuries. In 1996, he spun his first against the Colorado Rockies at Cooks field of all places.

All of these pitchers have manufactured two or more no-hitters during their careers. Nolan Ryan of course leads with seven, followed by Sandy Koufax who has four. Just a point of information: Ryan is the only one to pitch no-hitters in three different decades.

Of these pitchers, six of them threw two in the same season with Johnny Vander Meer fashioning his two in consecutive starts.

Pitchers with two or More No-Hitters Pitched

Cy Young

Home 1) 9/18/1892	Cleveland	6	Cincinnati	0
National League				
Home 2) 5/8/1904	Boston	3	Philadelphia	0
American League				

C. Mathewson

Away 1) 7/15/1901	New York	5	St. Louis	0
National League				
Away 2) 6/13/1905	New York	1	Chi	0
National League				
Away 3) 6/3/1908	Boston	8	New York	0
American League				

F. Smith

Away 1) 9/6/1905	Chicago	15	Detroit	0
American League				
Home 2) 9/20/1908	Chicago	1	Philadelphia	0
American League				

A. Joss

Home 1) 10/2/1908	Cleveland	1	Chicago	0
American League				
Away 2) 4/20/1910	Cleveland	1	Chicago	0
American League				

D. Leonard

Home 1) 8/30/1916	Cleveland	1	Chicago	0
American League				
Away 2) 6/03/1918	Boston	5	Detroit	0
American League				

J. Vander Meer

Home 1) 6/11/1938	Cincinnati	3	Boston	0
National League				

| Away | 2) 6/15/1938 | Cincinnati | 6 | Brooklyn | 0 |
| | National League | | | | |

B. Feller
Away	1) 4/16/1940	Cleveland	1	Chicago	0
	American League				
Away	2) 4/30/1946	Cleveland	1	New York	0
	American League				
Home	3) 7/1/1951	Cleveland	2	Detroit	1
	American League				

A. Reynolds
Away	1) 7/12/1951	New York	1	Cleveland	0
	American League				
Home	2) 9/28/1951	New York	8	Boston	0
	American League				

V. Trucks
Home	1) 5/18/1952	Detroit	1	Washington	0
	American League				
Away	2) 8/25/1952	Detroit	1	New York	0
	American League				

C. Erskine
Home	1) 6/19/1952	Brooklyn	5	Chicago	0
	National League				
Home	2) 5/12/1956	Brooklyn	3	New York	0
	National League				

W. Spahn
Home	1) 9/16/1960	Milwaukee	4	Philadelphia	0
	National League				
Home	2) 4/28/1960	Milwaukee	1	San Francisco	0
	National League				

S. Koufax

Home	1) 6/30/1962	Los Angeles	5	New York	0
	National League				
Home	2) 5/11/1963	Los Angeles	8	San Francisco	0
	National League				
Away	3) 6/4/1964	Los Angeles	3	Philadelphia	0
	National League				
Away	4) 9/9/1965	Los Angeles	1	Chicago	0

*Perfect Game

J. Bunning

Away	1) 7/20/1958	Detroit	3	Boston	0
	American League				
Away	2) 6/21/1964	Philadelphia	6	New York	0
	National League				

J. Maloney

Away	1) 8/19/1965	Cincinnati	1	Chicago	0
	National League				
Home	2) 9/30/1969	Cincinnati	1	Houston	0
	National League				

D. Wilson

Home	1) 4/17/1969	Montana	7	Philadelphia	0
	National League				
Away	2) 5/1/1969	Houston	4	Cincinnati	0
	National League				

K. Holtzman

Home	1) 8/19/1969	Chicago	3	Atlanta	0
	National League				
Home	2) 6/3/1971	Chicago	1	Cincinnati	0
	National League				

B. Stoneman

Away	1) 4/17/69	Montreal	7	Philadelphia	0
	National League				

Home	2) 10/2/72	Montreal	7	New York	0
	National League				

N. Ryan

Away	1) 5/15/1973	California	3	KC	0
	American League				
Away	2) 7/15/1973	California	6	Detroit	0
	American League				
Home	3) 9/28/1974	California	4	Minnesota	0
	American League				
Home	4) 6/1/1975	California	1	Baltimore	0
	American League				
Home	5) 9/26/1981	Houston	5	Los Angeles	0
	National League				
Away	6) 6/11/1990	Texas	5	Oakland	0
	American League				
Home	7) 5/1/1991	Texas	3	Toronto	0
	American League				

S. Busby

Away	1) 4/27/1973	KC	3	Detroit	0
	American League				
Away	2) 6/19/1974	KC	2	Milwaukee	0
	American League				

B. Forsch

Home	1) 4/16/1978	St. Louis	5	Philadelphia	0
	National League				
Home	2) 9/26/1978	St. Louis	3	Montreal	0
	National League				

H. Nomo

Away	1) 9/17/1996	Los Angeles	9	Colorado	0
	National League				
Away	2) 4/4/2001	Boston	3	Baltimore	0
	American League				

*Perfect game

Mark Buehrle

Home	1) 4/18/2007	Chicago	6	Texas	0
	American League				
Home	2) 7/23/2009	Chicago	5	Tampa Bay	0
	American League				

*Perfect game

Justin Verlander

Home	1) 6/12/2007	Detroit	4	Milwaukee	0
	Inter-League				
Away	2) 5/7/2011	Detroit	9	Toronto	0
	American				

Roy Halladay

Away	1) 5/29/2010	Philadelphia	1	Florida	0
	National				

*Perfect game

Home	2) 10/6/2010	Philadelphia	4	Cincinnati	0
	NLDS				

H. Bailey

Away	1) 9/28/2012	Cincinnati	1	Pittsburgh	0
	National League				
Home	2) 7/2/13	Cincinnati	3	San Francisco	0
	National League				

Tim Lincecum

Away	1) 7/13/2013	San Francisco	9	San Diego	0
	National League				
Home	2) 6/25/2014	San Francisco	4	San Diego	0
	National League				

Max Scherzer

Home	1) 6/20/2015	Washington	6	Pittsburgh	0
	National League				
Away	2) 10/3/2015	Washington	2	New York	0
	National League				

Jake Arrieta

Away 1) 8/30/2015 Chicago   2   Los Angeles   0
         National League
Away 2) 4/21/2016 Chicago   16   Cincinnati   0

Reigning CY Young Award Winners to throw a no-hitter

1964	Sandy Koufax	Los Angeles Dodgers
1971	Bob Gibson	St. Louis Cardinals
2014	Clayton Kershaw	Los Angeles Dodgers
2016	Jake Arrieta	Chicago Cubs

Only Pitcher with Two Decisions in a 300 Game Win.

On 6/2/1891, Charles "Old Hoss" Radbourn, while pitching for the Cincinnati Reds notched his 300th career victory. He defeated the Boston Beaneaters 10-8. The losing pitcher was John Clarkson.

The following year, Clarkson, now with the Cleveland Spiders, defeated the Pittsburgh Pirates on 9/21/1892 three to two. The significance of this was that Clarkson achieved his three hundredth career win, making him the only pitcher to appear in more than one three hundredth game victory. To this day, he is still the only one.

Teammates with No-Hitters in the Same Year.

Since 1900, there have been eight occasions when teammates on the same pitching staff twirled no-hit games in the same year. In 1917, the St. Louis Browns did it against the eventual world champion Chicago White Sox on consecutive days. This was not a consecutive game because the Brownies second no-hitter came in the second game of a double header.

For those pre 1900 buffs, no-hitters by teammates have happened three times.

American League   National League

1904 Boston   1956 Brooklyn
Cy Young vs. Philadelphia *   C. Erskine vs. New York
Jesse Tannehill vs. Chicago   S. Maglie vs. Philadelphia

1908 Cleveland   1960 Milwaukee
B. Rhoads vs. Boston   L. Burdette vs. Philadelphia
A. Joss vs. Chicago   W. Spahn vs. Philadelphia

1916 Boston   1972 Chicago
R. Foster vs. New York   B. Hooton vs. Philadelphia
D. Leonardo vs. St. Louis   M. Pappas vs. San Diego

1917 St. Louis
E. Koob vs. Chicago
(Consecutive days but not consecutive games.)
B. Groom vs. Chicago

1962 Boston   2014 Los Angeles
E. Wilson vs. Los Angles   J. Beckett vs. Philadelphia
B. Monbouquette vs. Chicago   C. Kershaw vs. Colorado

Pre 1900

American Association

1882 Louisiana   1884 Col
T. Mullane vs. Cincinnati   E. Morris vs. Pittsburgh
(first at 50 ft. distance)   F. Mountain vs. Washington
G. Hecker vs. Pittsburgh

1888 Philadelphia
E. Seward vs. Cincinnati
G. Weyhing vs. KC

ERA Leaders with an ERA of 3.00 or Greater.

It does not happen often when a pitcher tops the ERA list with a 3.00 or higher. This has happened only 6 times, with each league having done it three times.

American League		National League	
B. Grove 1938 Boston	3.07	R. Ryan 1922 New York	3.00
E. Wynn 1950 Cleveland	3.20	B. Walker 1929 New York	3.08
F. Garcia 2001 Seattle	3.05	W. Spahn 1961 Milwaukee	3.01
J. Lackey Los Angeles	3.01		

The Pitching Triple Crown Winners

Just as hitters have Triple Crown categories, pitchers also have theirs. This consists of wins, strikeouts and ERA. Grover Cleveland Alexander accomplished it four times. "Alex the Great" did it three consecutive years, being the only pitcher that achieved this.

American League

C. Young		1901		R. Waddell		1905
Wins	S.O.	ERA		Wins	S.O.	ERA
33	158	1.62		27	287	1.48

W. Johnson		1913		W. Johnson		1918
Wins	S.O.	ERA		Wins	S.O.	ERA
36	243	1.14		23	162	1.27

W. Johnson		1924		L. Grove		1930
Wins	S.O.	ERA		Wins	S.O.	ERA

23	158	2.72

28	209	2.54

L. Grove   1931

Wins	S.O.	ERA
31	175	2.06

L. Gomez   1934

Wins	S.O.	ERA
26	158	2.33

L. Gomez   1937

Wins	S.O.	ERA
21	194	2.33

B. Feller   1940

Wins	S.O.	ERA
27	261	2.61

H. Newhouser 1945

Wins	S.O.	ERA
25	212	1.81

R. Clemens   1997

Wins	S.O.	ERA
21	292	2.05

R. Clemens   1998

Wins	S.O.	ERA
20	271	2.65

P. Martinez   1999

Wins	S.O.	ERA
23	313	2.07

J. Santana   2006

Wins	S.O.	ERA
19	245	2.77

J. Verlander   2011

Wins	S.O.	ERA
24	250	2.40

National League

C. Mathewson 1905

Wins	S.O.	ERA
31	206	1.22

C. Mathewson 1908

Wins	S.O.	ERA
37	259	1.43

G. Alexander 1915

Wins	S.O.	ERA
31	241	1.22

G. Alexander 1916

Wins	S.O.	ERA
33	167	1.55

G. Alexander 1917

Wins	S.O.	ERA
30	201	1.86

H. Vaughn   1918

Wins	S.O.	ERA
22	148	1.74

G. Alexander		1920
Wins	S.O.	ERA
27	173	1.91

D. Vance		1924
Wins	S.O.	ERA
28	262	2.16

B. Walters		1939
Wins	S.O.	ERA
27	137	2.29

S. Koufax		1966
Wins	S.O.	ERA
25	306	1.88

S. Koufax		1965
Wins	S.O.	ERA
26	382	2.04

S. Koufax		1966
Wins	S.O.	ERA
27	317	1.73

S. Carlton		1972
Wins	S.O.	ERA
27	310	1.97

D. Gooden		1985
Wins	S.O.	ERA
24	268	1.53

J. Peavy		2007
Wins	S.O.	ERA
19	240	2.54

C. Kershaw		2011
Wins	S.O.	ERA
21	248	2.28

Pitchers That Won Twenty Games in Three Different Decades.

When Roger Clemens went 20-3 for the Yankees in 2001, he tied Warren Spahn as being the only pitcher who won twenty or more games in three different decades. While Spahn did it for one team (the Braves), Clemens achieved his feat with three different teams. Each will have the distinction of being the only one to do it in their respected leagues.

W. Spahn

Boston	National League	1947 & 1949
Boston	National League	1950 & 1951
Milwaukee	National League	1953, 1954, 1596-1959
Milwaukee	National League	1960, 1961 & 1963

R. Clemens

Boston	American League	1986 & 1987
Boston	American League	1990
Toronto	American League	1997 & 1998
New York	American League	2001

Pitchers with Two No-Hitters in the Same Season.

In 1938, Johnny Vander Meer became the first pitcher to toss two no-hitters in the same year. The uniqueness about it was that they were consecutive starts. "Vandy's" feat has never been duplicated, but there are five others who also pitched two no-hitters in the same year.

Allie Reynolds of the New York Yankees was the second to do it. The oddity about Reynolds second no-hitter was it clinched the pennant for the Yanks. The final out in that game was Ted Williams. Williams lifted a foul pop that catcher "Yogi" Berra dropped. Fate was with Reynolds as he got Williams to duplicate the at-bat, which Berra successfully caught.

The following year, Virgil Trucks of the Detroit Tigers twirled two no-hitters. His second was also of an unordinary type. Trucks gave an infield chopper early in the game that handcuffed short stop Johnny Pesky. The official scorer ruled a hit. As the game progressed into the late innings, the only hit was that infield chopper. The official scorer called down to the Tiger dugout and questioned Pesky about it. Pesky revealed that it was a ball he should have played. This was what the scorer needed to know and he reversed his decision there by giving Trucks a no-hitter.

October 6, 2010 in his first Post Season appearance Roy Halladay pitched a no-hitter in Game 1 of the NLDS. Halladay is only the second pitcher to pitch a no-hitter in the Post Season; the first being Don Larsen and his Perfect Game in the 1956 World Series.

American League

1951	A. Reynolds					
A	7/12	New York	vs.	Cleveland	1-0	
H	9/28	New York	vs.	Boston	8-0	
		(Clinched Pennant)				

1952	V. Trucks					
	5/15	Detroit	vs.	Washington	1-0	
A	8/25	Detroit	vs.	New York	1-0	

1973	N. Ryan					
	5/15	California	vs.	KC	3-0	
	7/15	California	vs.	Detroit	6-0	

National League

1938	J. Vander Meer				
	6/11	Cincinnati	vs.	Boston	3-0
	6/15	Cincinnati	vs.	Brooklyn	6-0
		(Consecutive)			

2010 R. Halladay					
	5/29	Philadelphia	vs.	Florida	1-0
	10/6	Philadelphia	vs.	Cincinnati	4-0

2015 M. Scherzer					
	6/20	Washington	vs.	Pittsburgh	6-0
	10/3	Washington	vs.	New York	2-0

<u>No-Hitter Pitchers with Two Different Leagues.</u>

In 1891, Ted Breitenstein, while pitching for the St. Louis Browns of the American Associations, no-hit the Louisville Colonels beating them 8-0, according to the Sporting News in their complete baseball record book. It was his first Major League start.

In 1898, he threw his second no-hitter when as a member of the Cincinnati Reds he defeated Pittsburgh 11-0. This made him the first man to pitch no-hitters in two different leagues. It also made him the only one to spin no-hitters at the present distance of 60' 6" and a previous distance of 50'.

Cy Young
National League	Cleveland 6-Cincinnati 0	1897
American League	Boston 4-Philadelphia 0	1904 (Perfect Game)
American League	Boston 8-New York 0	1908

Jim Bunning
| American League | Detroit 3-Boston 0 | 1958 |
| National League | Philadelphia 6-New York 0 | 1964 |

Hideo Nomo
| National League | Los Angles 9-Colorado 0 | 1996 |
| American League | Boston 4- Baltimore 0 | 2001 |

Nolan Ryan
American League	California 3-KC 0	1973
American League	California 6-Detroit 0	1973
American League	California 4-Minnesota 0	1974
American League	California 1-Baltimore 0	1975
National League	Houston 5-Los Angles 0	1981
American League	Texas 3-Toronto 0	1991
American League	Texas 5-Oakland 0	1990

Randy Johnson
| American League | Seattle 2-Detroit 0 | 1990 |
| National League | Arizona 5-Atlanta 0 | 2004 |

T. Breitenstein
American Association St. Louis 8-Louisiana 0	1891
(First Major League start)	
National League	Cincinnati 11-Pittsburgh 0

Pitchers Consecutive Win Streak Season.

In 1888, Tin Keefe set the all-time consecutive win streak for pitchers at nineteen in a season. This is the benchmark that has been aimed at, and only once has it been met. Rube Marquard reached nineteen in 1912. His was more remarkable than Keefe's because Marquard's endeavors were done at 60' 6" while Keefe has achieved his at 50' distance. Both pitchers were able to notch on their gun handle the name of their opponents. Marquard succeeded in doing that after his eighth victory.

In the American League, the record is sixteen straight victories. That was reached five times with Roger Clemens being the most recent in 2001.

The year 1912 seemed to be the year that record streaks were set. Walter Johnson set the AL record at sixteen. After Johnson won his second game in a row, Joe Wood followed suit. That would tie Johnson for the league record. By the time Wood had reached thirteen in a row, he was matched up against Johnson. In a classic duel of thirty game winners, Wood prevailed 1-0 to reach fourteen consecutive victories. Wood succeeded in his next two starts to tie Johnson.

The next time sixteen straight wins happened was in 1931, when Lefty Grove tied the record. His streak stopped when he lost one to zero on a misplayed fly ball by his left fielder. Grove destroyed his clubhouse in a fit of rage.

Three years later "School Boy" Rowe would take his share of the record. Rowe is the only one of the five American Leaguers to defeat his seven opponents in the streak. His last victory in the string game was against the Washington Senators, which was the only team in the streak that he did not defeat.

Tim Keefe 1888, Nineteen Games Win Streak.

				Hits	Loser
A	1. 6/23	Philadelphia	7-6	8	Casey

A	2. 6/26	Philadelphia	4-1	4	Casey
H	3. 6/29	Washington	8-3	4	Gilmore
H	4. 7/3	Washington	6-2	2	Gilmore
A	5. 7/4	Detroit	4-1	6	Getzien
A	6. 7/7	Pittsburgh	6-4	7	Morris
A	7. 7/11	Indiana	5-2	6	Healy
A	8. 7/13	Indiana	4-0	3	Boyle
A	9. 7/16	Chicago	12-4	5	Van Haltren
A	10. 7/17	Chicago	7-4	7	Krock
A	11. 7/20	Philadelphia	7-6	12	Casey
H	12. 7/23	Boston	2-0	3	Clarkson
H	13. 7/25	Boston	5-1	4	Sowders
H	14. 7/28	Philadelphia	4-2	7	Sanders
H	15. 8/1	Washington	5-4	6	Widner
H	16. 8/3	Boston	9-6	9	Sowders (Boston 9 hits, Keefe didn't finish)
H	17. 8/6	Indiana	3-2	7	Shreve
H	18. 8/8	Indiana	4-1	5	Boyle
H	19.8/10	Pittsburgh	2-1	4	Staley

Lost to Chicago in New York 4-2, gave up five hits, the winning pitcher was Krock.

Rube Marquard 1912, Nineteen Game Win Streaks.

Victory #		Date	Team	Score	Hits	Losing Pitcher
1	A	4/11	Brooklyn	18-3	7	N. Rucker
2	A	4/16	Boston	8-2	6	Tyler
3	A	4/24	Philadelphia	11-4	7	G. Alexander
4	H	5/1	Philadelphia	11-4	10	T. Seaton
5	A	5/7	St. Louis	6-2	6	Steele
6	A	5/11	Chicago	10-3	8	Richie
7	A	5/16	Pittsburgh	4-1	4	O'Toole
8	A	5/20	Cincinnati	3-0	6	Fromme
9	A	5/24	Brooklyn	6-3	8	Ragan
10	A	5/30	Philadelphia	7-1	9	T. Seaton
11	H	6/3	St. Louis	8-3	9	Sallee

12	H	6/8	Cincinnati	6-2	4	Fromme
13	H	6/12	Chicago	3-2	8	M. Brown
14	H	6/17	Pittsburgh	5-4	12	O'Toole
15	A*	6/19	Boston	6-5	1	Hess (Relief)
16	A	6/21	Boston	5-2	10	Perdue
17	H	6/25	Philadelphia	2-1	6	G. Alexander
18	H	6/29	Boston	8-6	11	Brown
19	H	7/3	Brooklyn	2-1	9	N. Rucker

Lost the away game 7/8/12 to Chicago 7-2, gave up eight hits, the winning pitcher was Lavender.

Walter Johnson 1912, Sixteen Games Win Streak.

Victory #		Date	Team	Score	Hits	Losing Pitcher
1	H	7/3	New York	10-2	6	Fisher
2	H	7/5	New York	6-5	4	Warhop (Relief 11 1/3- 15 innings)
3	H	7/9	Cleveland	4-3	8	Mitchell
4	H	7/13	Chicago	4-2	7	Cicotte
5	H	7/16	Chicago	7-2	7	Peters
6	H	7/22	Detroit	5-3	7	Works
7	H	7/25	Detroit	7-5	8	Mullins
8	A	7/28	Cleveland	4-1	8	Gregg
9	A	8/2	Detroit	4-0	7	Willet
10	A	8/5*	Chicago	8-7	0	White (Relief)
11	A	8/7	Chicago	10-1	2	Lange
12	A	8/11	St. Louis	3-2	4	Hamilton
13	H	8/15*	Chicago	4-3	2	Walsh (Relief)
14	H	8/16	Chicago	4-0	1	Benz
15	H	8/20	Cleveland	4-2	10	Steen
16	H	8/23	Detroit	8-1	7	Dubuc

Lost at home 8/28/1912, to St. Louis 3-2, gave up four hits and the winning pitcher was Powell.

Joe Wood 1912, Sixteen Game Win Streak .

Victory #		Date	Team	Score	Hits	Losing Pitcher

1	H	7/8	St. Louis	5-1	7	Allison
2	H	7/12	Detroit	1-0	5	Willet
3	H	7/17	Chicago	7-3	6	Peters
4	H	7/23	Cleveland	6-3	9	Blanding
5	A	7/28	Chicago	5-4	6	Cicotte
6	A	8/2	St. Louis	9-0	3	Hamilton
7	A	8/6	Cleveland	5-4	13	Blanding
8	A	8/10	Detroit	4-1	7	Willet
9	H	8/14	St. Louis	8-0	4	Allison
10	H	8/20	Detroit	6-2	6	Dubuc
11	H	8/24	Cleveland	8-4	7	Gregg
12	H	8/28	Chicago	3-0	6	Taylor
13	A	9/2	New York	1-0	8	McConnell
14	H	9/6	Washington	1-0	6	Johnson
15	A	9/10	Chicago	5-4	12	White
16	A	9/15	St. Louis	2-1	7	Hamilton

Lost away game on 9/20/12 against Detroit 6-4, gave up seven hits, winning pitcher was Lake.

Robert "Lefty" Grove Sixteen Game Winning Streak 1931

Victory #		Date	Team	Score	Hits	Losing Pitcher
1	H	6/8	Detroit	7-3	8	Whitehill
2	H	6/13	St. Louis	10-3	7	Stewart
3	A	6/19	Chicago	10-4	12	Caraway
4	A	6/23	St. Louis	3-0	2	Collins
5	A	6/27	Detroit	9-5	12	Herring
6	A	7/1	Cleveland	4-3	4	Ferrell
7	H	7/4	Boston	9-7	6	Morris
8	A	7/8	Washington	6-3	11	Brown
9	H	7/13	Washington	12-7	13	Hadley
10	H	7/17	Detroit	6-3	9	Uhle
11	H	7/25	Cleveland	6-3	8	Ferrell
12	H	7/28	St. Louis	6-3	0	Hebert
13	H	8/3	Washington	3-2	11	Jones
14	A	8/11	Detroit	8-1	8	Uhle
15	A	8/15	Cleveland	4-3	8	Ferrell

| 16 | A | 8/19/04 Chicago | 4-2 | 7 | Faber |

Lost away game on 8/24/31 to St. Louis 1-0, gave up seven hits, winning pitcher was Coffman.

School Boy Rowe Sixteen Game Winning Streak 1934

Victory #		Date	Team	Score	Hits	Losing Pitcher
1	A	6/15	Boston	11-4	9	Ostermueller
2	A	6/24	Philadelphia	8-4	12	Wilshere
3	A	7/1	St. Louis	12-3	13	Newsome
4	H	7/4*	Cleveland	5-2	4	Hudlin
5	H	7/8*	St. Louis	5-4	2	Newsome
6	H	7/12	New York	4-2	6	Broaca
7	H	7/15	New York	8-3	8	Murphy
8	H	7/22*	Philadelphia	17-8	6	Marcum
9	A	7/28	Chicago	11-1	3	Lyons
10	A	7/29*	Chicago	16-15	0	Heving
11	H	8/3	Chicago	14-0	1	Gaston
12	H	8/10	Cleveland	6-5	13	Harder
13	A	8/14	New York	7-3	4	Ruffing
14	A	8/17	New York	2-0	3	DeShong
15	A	8/21	Boston	8-4	9	Ostermueller
16	A	8/25	Washington	4-2	9	Weaver

Lost away game 8/29/34 to Philadelphia 13-5, gave up twelve hits, the winning pitcher was Marcum.

Roger Clemens Sixteen Game Winning Streak 2001

1	A	5/26	Cleveland	12-5	Sabathia
2	H	6/2	Cleveland	9-4	Colon
3	H	6/7	Baltimore	4-0	Ponson
4	H	6/13	Montreal	9-3	Irabu
5	A	6/18	Detroit	10-1	Weaver
6	A	6/23	T.B.	2-1	Wallace
7	H	6/29	T.B.	7-5	Rekar
8	A	7/4	Baltimore	4-3	Maduro
9	A	7/18	Detroit	8-5	Sparks

10	H	7/23	Toronto	7-2	Parris
11	A	7/28	Toronto	12-1	Escobar
12	H	8/15	T.B.	7-5	Valdes
14	A	8/31	Boston	3-1	Lowe
15	A	9/5	Toronto	4-3	Escobar
16	A	9/19	Chicago	6-3	Glover

Winning streak came to an end at T.B. as New York loses 4-0 to Sturtze.

Pitchers with Five Consecutive Shutouts.

In 1904, Guy "Doc" White became the first hurler to spin five consecutive shutouts. His fifth would be a significant one because he would defeat the New York Highlanders and Jack Chesbro, the Highlanders forty game winner. The Highlanders were in a dogfight with the Boston Americans for the pennant. At this stage of the season, every win for New York had special meaning. Winning their ace (Chesbro) would go on to set the modern record for wins in a season (41), was quite a task.

White's record would tumble sixty-four years later when Don Drysdale of the Los Angeles Dodgers would fashion six consecutive shutouts. The oddity in Drysdale's string of white washes was that an umpire's decision kept his streak going. In his fifth game against the San Francisco Giants, Drysdale had the bases loaded with two outs when apparently a pitch hit Dick Dietz. The umpire ruled that the batter did not attempt to get out of the way, thus nullifying the run that would have broken the streak. Drysdale eluded his jam and completed his shutout in his following start. He set the record at six.

Two days before Drysdale's streak ended, Bob Gibson of the St. Louis Cardinals made a strong challenge to the new record. He ripped off five consecutive shutouts and was aiming for his sixth straight. His opponents would be the Dodgers and opposing him on the mound would be none other but Drysdale. The drama of the game would end abruptly in the first inning. *With two outs, Los Angeles with a walk and a single.* A runner was on third when Gibson released his next pitch that bounced off of the catcher's mitt. This allowed the runner to score breaking Gibson string of shutouts. The pitch was ruled a wild pitch. Gibson went on to win five to one. His next start was another shutout. If not for that one pitch, Gibson might have had seven blankings in a row.

Drysdale's Six Consecutive Shutouts in 1968.

S.O. #	Date	Score	Team	Hits	B.B.	S.O.	Losing Pitcher
1	5/14	1-0	Chicago	2	3	7	F. Jenkins
2	5/18	1-0	Houston	5	2	6	D. Giusti
3	5/22	2-0	St. Louis	5	0	8	R. Gibson
4	5/26	5-0	Houston	6	2	6	L. Dierker
5	5/31	3-0	San Francisco	6	2	7	M. McCormick
6	6/4	5-0	Pittsburgh	3	0	8	J. Bunning

Drysdale's string of shutouts was broken on 6/8/68 when Philadelphia scored in the fifth inning. Drysdale was victorious in a 5-3 victory pitching six and a third innings.

Bob Gibson's Five Consecutive Shutouts 1968

S.O. #	Date	Score	Team	Hits	B.B.	S.O.	Losing Pitcher
1	6/6	5-0	Hou	3	2	5	D. Wilson
2	6/11	6-0	Atl	5	2	4	Kelley
3	6/15	2-0	Cin	4	0	13	G. Nolan
4	6/20	1-0	Chi	5	1	6	F. Jenkins
5	6/26	3-0	Pit	4	0	7	A. McBean

Gibson's string of shutouts was broken on 7/1/1968 when Los Angeles scored a run in the first inning. Gibson was victorious five to one pitching a complete game. The losing pitcher was Don Drysdale.

Guy "Doc" White Five Consecutive Shutouts 1904.

S.O. #	Date	Score	Team	Hits	B.B.	S.O.	Losing Pitcher
1	9/12	1-0	Cle	7	2	8	A. Joss
2	9/16	1-0	St. L	1	1	6	Siever
3	9/19	3-0	Det	2	3	4	Kitson

| 4 | 9/25 | 4-0 | Phi | 4 | 2 | 6 | A. Coakley |
| 5 | 9/30 | 4-0 | NY | 3 | 3 | 8 | J. Chesbro |

White's shutout string was broken on 10/2/04 when he gave up a run in the first inning to New York. White was victorious seven to one, pitching a complete game.

Orel Hershiser Five Consecutive Shutout 1988

				Hits	B.B.	S.O.	Losing Pitcher
1	9/5	Atlanta	3-0	4	1	8	Mahler
2	9/10	Cincinnati	5-0	7	3	8	Charlton
3	9/14	Atlanta	1-0	6	2	8	Mahler
4	9/19	Houston	1-0	4	0	5	Darwin
5	9/23	San Francisco	3-0	5	2	1	Hammaker

Ed Reulbach Day of Two Shutouts.

Several times in the early years of the twentieth century, pitchers would start both games of a doubleheader. Many completed and won both, but only once did a pitcher spin shutouts in both games. This unparalleled feat was turned in by the Chicago Cubs' Ed Reulbach during the heat of the 1908 pennant race. Manager Frank Chance asked Reulbach to do Yeoman's duty by taking the mound in both games. Ed obliged and the rest is history. The effect of the doubleheader did not bother Ed as he improved as he went along. He gave up seven hits in the opener and was more effective in the nightcap when he scattered three hits.

Two Shutout Victories in One Day

	Game	Team	Score	Hits	B.B.	S.O.	Losing Pitcher
9/26/1908	1	Brooklyn	5-0	5	0	7	Wilhelm
	2	Brooklyn	3-0	3	1	4	Pastorius

Rookie Teammates Who Were Twenty Game Winners.

When a team obtains a pitcher who wins twenty games in his rookie year, it is like finding a diamond in the rough. Only once in baseball history has a team been blessed with two rookies who made the charmed circle of twenty wins. This occurred in 1937, when the Boston Braves brought up Jim Turner and Lou Fette.

The Braves in 1936 finished sixth with a below .500 percentage. With Turner and Fette, they moved up a notch with a percentage above .500. Besides winning twenty games each, they both led the league in shutouts. Turner also captured the ERA crown. It would not have been surprising to notice gray hair under their caps. Turner was thirty-three and Fette was thirty in their freshman year.

1937 Boston National League
Lou Fette   20-10   Age 30
Jim Turner   20-11   Age 33
Both lead the league in shutouts. Turner led in ERA.

Pitchers Who Had a Twenty Win Season For Three or More Teams.

In 1903, Joe McGinnity did something that never was done before in baseball history while pitching for the New York Giants. He topped the twenty-win mark for his fourth team. The following year, Jack Powell while pitching for the New York Highlander duplicated McGinnity's feat. Five others won 20 for three different teams. Listed are those pitchers.

J. McGinnity
1899 Baltimore   National League   28-17
1900 Brooklyn   National League   29-9
1901 Brooklyn   National League   29-9
1903 New York   National League   31-20
1904 New York   National League   35-8
1905 New York   National League   21-15
1906 New York   National League   27-12

J. Powell
1898 Cleveland   National League   23-15
1899 St. Louis   National League   23-21

1902 St. Louis	National League	23-21
1906 New York	American League	23-19

C. Young

1981 Cleveland	National League	27-20
1892 Cleveland	National League	36-11
1893 Cleveland	National League	32-16
1894 Cleveland	National League	25-22
1895 Cleveland	National League	35-10
1896 Cleveland	National League	29-16
1897 Cleveland	National League	21-18
1898 Cleveland	National League	25-14
1899 St. Louis	National League	26-15
1900 St. Louis	National League	20-18
1901 Boston	American League	33-10
1902 Boston	American League	32-11
1903 Boston	American League	28-9
1904 Boston	American League	26-16
1907 Boston	American League	22-15
1908 Boston	American League	21-11

G. Alexander

1911 Philadelphia	National League	28-13
1913 Philadelphia	National League	22-8
1914 Philadelphia	National League	27-15
1915 Philadelphia	National League	31-10
1916 Philadelphia	National League	33-12
1917 Philadelphia	National League	30-13
1920 Chicago	National League	27-14
1923 Chicago	National League	22-12
1927 St. Louis	National League	21-10

C. Mays

1917 Boston	American League	22-9
1918 Boston	American League	21-13
1920 New York	American League	26-11

1921 New York	American League	27-9
1924 Cincinnati	National League	20-9

G. Perry

1966 San Francisco	National League	21-8
1972 Cleveland	American League	24-16
1974 Cleveland	American League	21-13
1978 San Diego	National League	21-6

R. Clemens

1986 Boston	American League	24-4
1987 Boston	American League	20-9
1990 Boston	American League	21-6
1997 Toronto	American League	21-7
1998 Toronto	American League	20-6
2001 New York	American League	20-3

Teams with Three Infielders Leading in Errors in the Same Year.

This only happened six times in modern history with the Anaheim Angels becoming the last team to do it in 2000. In 1916, the Philadelphia Phillies were the first team to in history to create this undistinguished mark of ineptness. Those three infielders had committed one hundred thirty-seven errors. Add third baseman Milt Stock and you have the whopping total of one hundred fifty-three.

Leading League in Errors Three Infielders on the Same Team.

American League

1971 Chicago		1996 Milwaukee		2000 Ana	
1B C. Mays	18	2B F. Vina	116	1B M. Vaughn	14
2B M. Andrews	17	SS J. Valentin	37	2B A. Kennedy	19
SS L. Richards	26	3B J. Cirillo	18	3B T. Glaus	37

Total	61	Total	71	Total	70

National League

1916 Philadelphia		1920 St. Louis		1988 Atlanta	
1B F. Luderus	28	1B J. Fournier	25	1B G. Perry	17
2B B. Niehoff	49	2B R. Hornsby	34	2B R.Gant	26
SS D. Bancroft	60	SS D. Lavan	50	SS A.Thomas	29
Total	137	Total	109	Total	72

Leading the League in Errors Double Play Combinations in the Same Year.

This has happened nineteen times since 1900, and is almost evenly distributed in both leagues. Surprisingly, three pennant winners are part of the list. Three of the combos surpassed the century mark in error. Let us speculate for a moment about the 1916 Philadelphia Phillies and the 1938 New York Yankees. With the 1916 Phillies having over 100 errors that might have been the reason they just missed having consecutive pennants. The case with the 1938 New York Yankees is the high total of errors might have been why they could not squeeze out one more victory to gain one hundred wins that season. One more win would have made it possible in gaining four consecutive one hundred win seasons.

Teams with Second Base and Short Stop Leading in Errors in the Same Year.

American League

1905 Washington		1907 St. Louis		1931 St. Louis	
2B C. Hickman	38	2B H. Niles	34	2B O. Melillo	32
SS J. Cassidy	66	SS B. Wallace	54	SS J. Levey	58
Total	104	Total	88	Total	90

1938 New York		1957 Detroit		1971 Chicago	
2B J. Gordon	31	2B F. Bolling	16	2B M. Andrews	17
SS F. Crosetti	47	SS H. Kuenn	27	SS L. Richard	26
Total	78	Total	43	Total	43

1984 Cleveland		1987 Seattle		1996 Milwaukee	
2B T. Bernazard	20	2B H. Reynolds	20	2B F. Vina	16
SS J. Franco	36	SS R. Quinones	25	SS J. Valentin	37
Total	56	Total	45	Total	53

National League

1908 New York		1916 Philadelphia		1920 St. Louis	
2B L. Doyle	33	2B B. Niehoff	49	2B R. Hornsby	34
SS A. Bridwell	35	SS D. Bancroft	60	SS D. Lavan	50
Total	68	Total	109	Total	84

1940 Pittsburgh		1949 Chicago		1952 Philadelphia	
2B F. Gustine	43	2B E. Verban	17	2B C. Ryan	23
SS F. Vaughn	52	SS R. Smalley	39	SS G. Hammer	38
Total	95	Total	56	Total	61

1964 St. Louis		1974 Los Angeles		1988 Atlanta	
2B J. Javier	27	2B D. Lopes	24	2B R. Gant	26
SS D. Groat	40	SS B. Russell	39	SS A. Thomas	29
Total	67	Total	63	Total	55

2001 Florida	
2B L. Castillo	13
SS A. Gonzalez	26
Total	39

The Only Man to Win the Fielding Title at Three Different Positions.

Not known for his glove but for his versatility, Pete Rose as of now can claim the distinction of being the only player to lead the league in fielding at three different positions.

| Cincinnati | 1970 | Outfielder | .997 |

| Cincinnati | 1976 | Third Base | .969 |
| Philadelphia | 1980 | First Base | .997 |

Players Who Led Their League at Three Different Positions in Errors.

Only two players can claim that undistinguished feat. They are Charles "Piano Legs" Hickman and Frank Gustine. Hickman spread his versatile misplaying with three different teams. Gustine on the other hand did his consistency of errors all with the Pittsburgh Pirates. He brought along the same glove wherever he played.

C. Hickman

1900	New York	National League	3B	86
1902	Cleveland	American League	1B	40
1903	Cleveland	American League	1B	40
1905	Washington	American League	2B	38

F. Gustine

1940	Pittsburgh	National League	2B	43
1945	Pittsburgh	National League	SS	35
1947	Pittsburgh	National League	3B	31

The Last Teams with Two Outfielders with Twenty Plus Assists.

One of the teams is The Boston Red Sox in 1935, and unbelievably, the San Diego Padres, and both are the last National League teams to achieve this.

American League		National League	
Boston 1935		San Diego 1980	
M. Almada	22	G. Richards	21
R. Johnson	21	D. Winfield	20

Teams with Three Outfielders Having Twenty or More Assists Each in the Same Season.

This only happened ten times since 1900. The Boston Red Sox

dominated this achievement six out of eight times in the American league. They did it five consecutive years (1910-1914). In 1912, the New York Giants also had their three gardeners amass twenty plus assists each. Imagine all six starting outfielders with twenty or more assists in the same World Series.

American League

1910 Bos		1911 Bos		1912 Bos	
H. Hooper	30	H. Hooper	27	H. Hooper	22
T. Speaker	20	T. Speaker	26	T. Speaker	35
D. Lewis	28	D. Lewis	27	D. Lewis	23

1913 Bos		1913 St. L		1914 Bos	
H. Hooper	25	G. Williams	26	H. Hooper	23
T. Speaker	30	B. Shotton	29	T. Speaker	29
D. Lewis	29	J. Johnston	23	D. Lewis	22

1916 Cle		1917 Bos	
B. Roth	20	H. Hooper	20
T. Speaker	25	T. Walker	20
J. Graney	22	D. Lewis	20

National League

1911 Cin		1912 NY	
M. Mitchell	23	R. Murray	20
J. Bates	21	B. Becker	20
B. Bescher	21	F. Snodgrass	25

Outfielders with 30 or More Assists in a Season.

Since the dawn of the twentieth century, there have been 34 occasions that an outfielder has assisted in gunning down base runners 30 or more times in a season. The majority of them were during the dead ball era. In fact the last American league outfield to aid in nailing 30 or more base runners was the great hitter Harry Heilmann in 1924 for Detroit. In the National League, Gene Moore was the last to assist in getting 30 plus runner and he did that in 1936. The only two men to have consecutive years of 30 plus assists were Tris Speaker in the American League and Benny Kauff in the Federal League. Only once in the history of the game did an outfielder have 40 plus assists in a year. This makes for a stellar trivia question. The answer is Chuck Klein who had 44 assists for the Phillies back in 1930. It looked as if Klein knew how to utilize that short right field defensively as well as offensively. That was also the year he had 250 hits.

American League					National League			
1901	J. Barrett	Det	31		1902	P. Donovan	St.L	30
1906	H. Niles	St.L	34		1903	J. Sheckard	Brl	36
1907	T. Cobb	Det	30		1907	M. Mitchell	Cin	39
1909	T. Speaker	Bos	35		1907	G. Beaumont	Bos	30
1910	C. Milan	Was	30		1909	R. Murray	NY	30
1910	H. Hooper	Bos	30		1911	J. Sheckard	Chi	32
1911	D. Murphy	Phi	34		1914	G. Cravath	Phi	34
1911	C. Kilan	Was	33		1914	D. Wilson	St.L	34
1911	J. Jackson	Cle	32		1916	M. Carey	Pit	32
1912	T. Speaker	Bos	35		1917	C. Stengel	Brk	30
1912	C. Milan	Was	31		1930	C. Klein	Phi	44
1912	J. Jackson	Cle	30		1936	G. Moore	Bos	32
1913	T. Speaker	Bos	30					
1914	T. Walker	St.L	30					
1917	F. Brodie	Phi	32					
1919	H. Felsch	Chi	32					
1923	I. Flagstead	Bos	33					
1924	H. Heilmann	Det	31					

Federal League

1914	C. Chadbourne	KC	34
1914	J. Tobin	St.L	31
1914	B. Kauff	Ind	31
1915	B. Kauff	Brk	32

Players Who Have Led Their Position in Fielding and Errors in the Same Year

This irony has happened twice in Major League history. Both times, it has occurred in the American League. In 1936, Tigers second baseman Charlie Gehringer topped the league in fielding .974 and in errors 25. Boston Red Sox third baseman Frank Malzone in 1957 won the fielding crown .954 and made the most errors at 25.

Fielding leader and error leader in the same year
2B. C. Gehringer   1936
3B. F. Malzone   1957

Teams with Three Infielders Leading in Fielding Percentage

In 1999, The New York Mets had such an airtight infield that three members lead the league in fielding percentage. Only John Olerud, who was always sure handed, failed to make it a complete sweep for the first time in Major League history. It would be the first time since 1964 that a Major League team would have three percentage leaders in their infield. It would be the first time a National League team would accomplish the feat since 1950.

AL

1905 Chi	1907 Cle	1923 NY
1B J. Donahue	2B N. Lajoie	2B A. Ward
2B G. Dundon	3B B. Bradley	3B J. Dungan
SS G. Davis	SS T. Turner	SS E. Scott
1932 Phi	1937 Det	1940 St. L
1B J. Foxx	2B C. Gehringer	1B G. McQuinn
2B M. Bishop	3B M. Owen	2B D. Heffner
3B J. Dykes	SS W. Rogell	3B H. Cliff
1962 Chi	1963 Bal	1964 Bal
1B J. Cunningham	1B J. Gentile	2B J. Adair
2 B N. Fox	3B B. Robinson	3B B. Robinson
SS L. Aparicio	SS L. Aparicio	SS L. Aparicio

NL

1902 Bos	1944 St. L	1950 Brk
1B F. Tenney	1B R. Sanders	1B G. Hodges
3B E. Gremminger	3B W. Kurowski	2B J. Robinson
SS H. Long	SS M. Marion	3B B. Cox

1999 (no name written)
2B E. Alfonso
3B R. Ventura
SS R. Ordonez

Teams in Each League to Have Less Than 100 Errors

In 1963, the Baltimore Orioles became the first Major League team to make fewer than 100 errors. They were a whisker under the century mark with 99. In the National League, the Cincinnati Reds became the first Senior Circuit team to break the 100 barrier. They committed only 95 in 1977.

AL			NL		
1963	Bal	99	1977	Cin	95
1964	Bal	95	1992	St. L.	94
1972	Det	96	1992	Cin	96
1980	Bal	95	1998	Atl	91
1987	Min	98	1999	NY	68
1988	Min	84	2000	SF	93
1988	Bos	93	2000	Col	94
1989	Cal	96	2001	Phi	91
1990	Tor	86	2002	Hou	83
1990	Oak	87	2002	Phi	88
1991	Bal	91	2002	Ari	89
1991	Min	95	2002	LA	90
1992	Mil	89	2002	SF	90
1992	Tor	93	2003	Stl	77
1992	Min	95	2003	Fla	78
1993	Sea	90	2003	SF	80
1993	KC	97	2003	Hou	95
1996	Tex	87	2003	Phi	97

1996	NY	91	2004	LA	73
1996	Min	94	2004	Phi	81
1996	Bal	97	2004	Chi	86
1997	KC	91	2004	Fla	86
1997	Det	92	2004	Col	89
1997	Tor	94	2004	Stl	97
1997	Bal	97	2004	Mon	99
1998	Bal	81	2005	Atl	86
1998	TB	94	2005	Hou	89
1998	NY	98	2005	Phi	90
1999	Bal	89	2005	SF	90
1999	Min	92	2005	Was	92
2000	Cle	72	2005	Ari	94
2000	Sea	99	2006	Hou	80
2001	Sea	83	2006	Col	91
2001	Tor	97	2006	SF	91
2002	Min	74	2006	SD	92
2002	Ana	87	2006	Stl	98
2002	Sea	88	2006	Atl	99
2002	Bal	91	2007	Col	68
2002	Chi	97	2007	Pit	83
2002	Tex	99	2007	SF	88
2003	Sea	65	2007	Phi	89
2003	Min	87	2007	Chi	94
2003	Chi	93	2007	SD	94
2003	Tex	94	2007	Cin	95
2004	Ana	90	2008	Hou	67
2004	Oak	91	2008	NY	83
2004	Tor	91	2008	SD	85
2004	NY	99	2008	Stl	85
2005	Sea	86	2008	Phi	90
2005	LA	87	2008	Col	96
2005	Oak	88	2008	SF	96
2005	Chi	94	2008	Chi	99
2005	NY	95	2009	Pit	73
2005	Tor	95	2009	Phi	76
2006	Bos	66	2009	Hou	78

2006	Min	84	2009	LA	83
2006	Oak	84	2009	Col	87
2006	Sea	88	2009	SF	88
2006	Chi	90	2009	Cin	89
2006	KC	98	2009	SD	94
2006	Tex	98	2009	Atl	96
2006	Tor	99	2009	Stl	96
2007	Bal	79	2009	NY	97
2007	Bos	81	2009	Mil	98
2007	NY	88	2010	Cin	72
2007	Oak	90	2010	SD	72
2007	Sea	90	2010	SF	73
2007	Cle	92	2010	Phi	83
2007	Min	96	2010	NY	87
2007	Det	99	2010	LA	98
2008	NY	83	2010	Stl	99
2008	Tor	84	2011	Phi	74
2008	Bos	85	2011	Atl	83
2008	TB	90	2011	LA	85
2008	LA	91	2011	Cin	91
2008	Cle	94	2011	Fla	93
2008	KC	96	2011	SD	94
2008	Oak	98	2011	Col	98
2008	Sea	99	2012	Atl	86
2009	Min	76	2012	Cin	89
2009	Tor	76	2012	Ari	90
2009	Bos	82	2012	Was	94
2009	LA	85	2012	LA	98
2009	NY	86	2012	Mil	99
2009	Det	88	2013	Ari	75
2009	Bal	90	2013	Stl	75
2009	Cle	97	2013	Cin	76
2009	TB	98	2013	SD	83
2010	NY	69	2013	Atl	85
2010	Min	78	2013	Mia	88
2010	TB	85	2013	Col	90
2010	Tor	92	2013	NY	93

2010	Oak	99	2013	Phi	97
2011	TB	73	2014	Cin	72
2011	Chi	79	2014	Phi	83
2011	Bos	92	2014	Atl	85
2011	LA	93	2014	Stl	88
2011	KC	95	2014	Mia	97
2012	Chi	70	2014	Mil	99
2012	Sea	72	2015	LA	75
2012	NY	75	2015	Mia	77
2012	Tex	85	2015	SF	78
2012	Cle	96	2015	Ari	86
2012	LA	98	2015	NY	88
2012	Det	99	2015	Cin	90
2013	Bal	54	2015	Was	90
2013	TB	59	2015	Atl	90
2013	NY	69	2015	SD	92
2013	Det	76	2015	Col	95
2013	Bos	80	2015	Stl	96
2013	Min	81			
2013	KC	85			
2013	Tex	86			
2013	Sea	88			
2013	Oak	97			
2013	Cle	98			
2014	Sea	82			
2014	LA	83			
2014	Bal	87			
2014	Tor	87			
2014	TB	88			
2014	Bos	92			
2014	NY	92			
2014	Min	97			
2015	Bal	77			
2015	Cle	79			
2015	Hou	85			
2015	Det	86			
2015	Min	86			

2015	KC	88
2015	Tor	88
2015	LA	93
2015	NY	93
2015	Sea	94
2015	TB	95
2015	Bos	97

First Baseman Fielding Records

Most Times Leading League in Fielding
   Three players managed to win the title seven times each. Don Mattingly has that distinction in the American League. Ed Konetchy and Charlie Grimm share the record in the National League. Regardless what some record books state, Grimm having nine titles is erroneous. Only seven titles can be verified. Listed are percentages and error committees. Notice that Konetchy won his titles with four different teams.

D. Mattingly

Yr.	Team	Per.	Errors
1984	NY	.996	5
1985	NY	.995	7
1986	NY	.996	6
1987	NY	.996	5
1992	NY	.997	4
1993	NY	.998	3
1993	NY	.998	2

E. Konetchy

Yr.	Team	Per	Errors
1910	St. L.	.991	15
1911	St. L.	.991	16
1913	St. L.	.995	7
1914	Pit	.995	8
1917	Bos	.994	8
1918	Bos	.992	11
1919	Brk	.994	9

C. Gehringer

Yr.	Team	Per.	Errors
1920	Pit	.995	8
1923	Pit	.995	8
1924	Pit	.995	8
1928	Chi	.993	10
1930	Chi	.995	6
1931	Chi	.993	10

1933   Chi   .996   4

Most Teams Leading Major League in Errors
This is a three-way tie between Hal Chase, Dick Stuart and Moe Vaughn at seven. Vaughn holds the American League record at six, while Stuart hold the National League record at five. Chase, by the way, has lead three leagues in errors. Chase was known as probably the shadiest player in the game's history and often threw games by committing errors purposely.

H. Chase	D. Stuart	M. Vaughn
1905 NY AL 31	1958 Pit NL 16	1992 Bos AL 15
1909 NY AL 28	1959 Pit NL 22	1993 Bos AL 16
1911 NY AL 36	1960 Pit NL 14	1994 Bos AL 10
1912 NY AL 27	1961 Pit NL 21	1996 Bos AL 15
1913 NY AL 33	1962 Pit NL 17	1997 Bos AL 14
1915 Buf FL 26	1963 Bos AL 29	2000 Ana AL 14
1917 Cin NL 28	1964 Bos AL 24	2002 NY NL 18

NL   Percentage Leader 1B

E. Konetchy				C. Grimm			
1910	St. L.	.991	15	1920	Pit	.995	8
1911	St. L.	.991	16	1923	Pit	.995	8
1913	St. L.	.995	7	1924	Pit	.995	8
1914	Pit	.995	8	1928	Chi	.993	10
1915	Pit	.994	10	1930	Chi	.995	6
1917	Bos	.994	8	1931	Chi	.993	10
1918	Bos	.992	11	1933	Chi	.996	4
1919	Brk	.994	9				

T. Kluszewski				W. Parker			
1951	Cin	.997	5	1965	LA	.997	5
1952	Cin	.993	8	1967	LA	.996	4
1953	Cin	.995	7	1968	LA	.999	1
1954	Cin	.996	5	1970	LA	.996	7
1955	Cin	.995	8	1972	LA	.997	4

S. Garvey
1975	LA	.995	8
1976	LA	.998	3
1977	LA	.995	8
1981	LA	.991	1
1984	SD	1.000	0

AL Percentage Leader 1B

J. McInnis					J. Judge			
1913	Phi	.992	13		1923	Was	.993	8
1914	Phi	.995	7		1925	Was	.993	7
1918	Bos	.992	9		1927	Was	.996	6
1920	Bos	.996	7		1929	Was	.996	6
1921	Bos	.999	1		1930	Was	.998	2
1922	Cle	.997	5					

D. Mattingly
1984	NY	.996	5
1985	NY	.995	7
1986	NY	.996	6
1987	NY	.996	5
1992	NY	.997	5
1993	NY	.998	3
1994	NY	.998	2

American League		Error Leaders		First Base		
H. Chase			G. Sisler		F. Fain		
1905	New York	31	1916	St. Louis 24	1947	Philadelphia	19
1909	New York	28	1917	St. Louis 22	1948	Philadelphia	16
1911	New York	36	1924	St. Louis 23	1949	Philadelphia	22
1912	New York	27	1925	St. Louis 26	1950	Philadelphia	19
1913	New York	33	1927	St. Louis 24	1952	Philadelphia	22
	Chicago						

First Baseman with 1800 Plus Total Chances

This only happened four times with three men doing it. Jiggs Donahue in 1907 missed by two getting the 2000 mark. This is indicative of the dead ball ERA where fielders have higher totals in every category than modern players.

American League				National League			
1906	J. Donahue	1,937		1920	G. Kelly	NY	1,873
1907	J. Donahue	1,998		1926	W. Pipp	Cin	1,817

1700 Put Outs

1907	J. Donahue	Chi	1,946	1920	G. Kelly	NY	1,739
1926	P. Todt	Bos	1,755	1926	W. Pipp	Cin	1,710

1800 Total Chances

American League				National League			
1906	J. Donahue	1,837		1920	G. Kelly	NY	1,873
1907	J. Donahue	1,998		1926	W. Pipp	Cin	1,817

Third Base Error Leaders

The record for leading the league in miscues at third base is five. It is also shared by two men, one in each league, with Hall of Famer 'Pie" Traynor holding the National League record. Traynor, known for his hitting, was usually listed as the third baseman on all-time teams. With men like Brooke Robinson and Mike Schmidt, Traynor's name has since been forgotten.

American League
J. Tabor

Year	Team	Errors
1939	Boston	40
1940	Boston	33
1941	Boston	30
1942	Boston	33
1943	Boston	26

National League

	P. Traynor	
Year	**Team**	**Errors**
1926	Pittsburgh	23
1928	Pittsburgh	27
1931	Pittsburgh	37
1932	Pittsburgh	27
1933	Pittsburgh	27

Third Baseman with 600 or More Chances in a Season

This has only happened eight times in the game's history. The major league record was set in 1904 by Tommy Leach with Pittsburgh. The last time that it was done was when Clete Boyer and Ron Santo did it.

American League

1911	J. Austin	St. Louis	607
1916	O. Vitt	Detroit	615
1937	H. Clift	St. Louis	637
1962	C. Boyer	New York	605

National League

1904	T. Leach	Pittsburgh	643
1907	B. Byrne	St. Louis	609
1909	B. Byrne	St. Louis/ Pittsburgh	610
1967	R. Santo	Chicago	606

Third Baseman with 200 or More Put Outs in a Season

This has been done thirty-six times through the years. The interesting thing is that it has not been done since 1956.

American League: done nineteen times, record set by W. Kamm at 243 with Chicago in 1929. Last time this was accomplished: 1952, by E. Yost with Washington at 212.

National League: done seventeen times, league record set by P. Traynor at 226 with Pittsburgh. Last time this was accomplished: 1956, by W. Jones with Philadelphia at 202.

Third Baseman with 400 or More Assists in a Season

Only three names will appear on this list. All three are household names that played the hot corner during the 1960's and 1970's.

American League

Year	Name	Team	Assists
1967	B. Robinson	Baltimore	405
1973	G. Nettles	Cleveland	412
1973	G. Nettles	New York	410
1974	B. Robinson	Baltimore	410

National League

Year	Name	Team	Assists
1974	M. Schmidt	Philadelphia	404

Short Stop Fielding Records

Most Times Leading League in Fielding

The number is eight shared by four men, of which three are enshrined in Cooperstown. Those three are noted for their fielding exploits. Two of the four won their title in eight consecutive years. Lou Boudreau, who won eight titles, in all probability would have coped nine titles all consecutively if he did not break his ankle in 1945. Notice that with the introduction of artificial turf the low totals of errors for the "Wizard of Oz." Regardless of the surface, he would have been a wizard if he played on a rock pile.

American League

E. Scott				L. Boudreau			
Year	Team	%	Errors	Year	Team	%	Errors
1916	Boston	.967	19	1940	Cleveland	.968	24
1917	Boston	.953	39	1941	Cleveland	.966	26

1918	Boston	.976	17		1942	Cleveland	.965	26
1919	Boston	.976	17		1943	Cleveland	.970	25
1920	Boston	.973	23		1944	Cleveland	.978	19
1921	Boston	.972	26		1946	Cleveland	.970	22
1922	New York	.966	30		1947	Cleveland	.978	14
1923	New York	.961	27		1948	Cleveland	.975	20

L. Aparicio

Year	Team	%	Errors
1959	Chicago	.970	23
1960	Chicago	.979	18
1961	Chicago	.962	30
1962	Chicago	.973	20
1963	Baltimore	.983	12
1964	Baltimore	.979	15
1965	Baltimore	.971	20
1966	Baltimore	.978	17

National League

J. Tinker

Year	Team	%	Errors
1906	Chicago	.944	45
1908	Chicago	.958	34
1909	Chicago	.940	50
1911	Chicago	.937	55
1913	Cincinnati	.968	18

E. Miller

Year	Team	%	Errors
1940	Boston	.970	28
1941	Boston	.966	29
1942	Boston	.983	13
1943	Cincinnati	.979	19
1945	Cincinnati	.975	27

L. Bowa

Year	Team	%	Errors
1971	Philadelphia	.987	11
1972	Philadelphia	.987	9
1974	Philadelphia	.984	12
1978	Philadelphia	.986	10
1979	Philadelphia	.991	6
1983	Chicago	.984	11

O. Smith

Year	Team	%	Errors
1981	San Diego	.976	16
1982	St. Louis	.984	13
1984	St. Louis	.982	12
1985	St. Louis	.983	14
1986	St. Louis	.978	15
1987	St. Louis	.987	10
1991	St. Louis	.987	8
1994	St. Louis	.982	8

Short Stop Error Leaders

The major league record is six shared by two men. In the American League, five is the most. *Years leading the league in errors:*

National League

D. Groat			R. Ramirez		
1955	Pittsburgh	32	1981	Atlanta	30
1956	Pittsburgh	34	1982	Atlanta	38
1959	Pittsburgh	29	1983	Atlanta	39
1961	Pittsburgh	32	1984	Atlanta	30
1962	Pittsburgh	38	1985	Atlanta	32
1964	St. Louis	40	1989	Houston	30

American League

Luke Appling

1933	Chicago	55
1935	Chicago	39
1937	Chicago	49
1939	Chicago	39
1946	Chicago	39

Short Stops with 1000 or More Total Chances in a Season

It has happened seven times by five different men, most of the time during the dead ball ERA. The last time it occurred was in 1926. Total chances are put outs, assists and errors added together.

American League

1908	H. Wagner	Boston	1,003
1911	D. Bush	Detroit	1,003
1914	D. Bush	Detroit	1,027

National League

1914	R. Maranville	Boston	1,046
1920	D. Bancroft	New York	1,005

1922	D. Bancroft	New York	1,046
1926	T. Thevenow	St. Louis	1,013

Short Stops with 400 or More Put Outs in a Season

This is a very short list of four. The most recent occurrence was in 1940.

American League	National League		
1914 D. Bush Detroit 425	1914 R. Maranville Boston	407
	1922 D. Bancroft New York	405
	1940 E. Miller Boston	405

Short Stops with 600 or More Assists in a Season

This has happened only twice, both times in the National League. Ozzie Smith set the all time record in 1980 with San Diego. This shows why he is the "Wizard."

American League	National League	
Never accomplished	1924 G. Wright Pittsburgh	601
	1980 O. Smith San Diego	621

Catcher Fielding Records

Catcher Leading League in Fielding

The record is six times once in the American League and once in the National League.

American League				National League			
J. Sundberg				G. Hartnett			
Year	Team	%	Errors	Year	Team	%	Errors
1976	Texas	.991	7	1928	Chicago	.989	6
1977	Texas	.994	5	1930	Chicago	.989	8

1978	Texas	.997	3		1934	Chicago	.996	3
1979	Texas	.995	4		1936	Chicago	.991	5
1984	Milwaukee	.995	3		1937	Chicago	.996	2
1986	KC	.995	4		1938	Chicago	.995	2

Catchers Who Are Credited with 1.000 Fielding Average
(100+ games Caught)

American League
1946 B. Rosar Philadelphia

National League
1997 C. Johnson Florida
2003 M. Matheny St Louis

Highest Fielding Average (150+ games Caught)

American League
1979 J. Sunderg Texas .995

National League
1967 R. Hundley Chicago .996

Catchers Leading the League in Errors Most Times

The major league record is seven by Ivey Wingo. In the American League, "Birdie" Tebbetts has the American League record at six.

American League
B. Tebbetts

1939	Detroit	16
1940	Detroit	17
1942	Detroit	12
1947	Detroit/Boston	10
1948	Boston	10
1949	Boston	11

National League
C. Dooin   I. Wingo

1902	Philadelphia	29		1912	Brooklyn	23
1904	Philadelphia	37		1913	St. Louis	28
1906	Philadelphia	32		1916	Cincinnati	28
1908	Philadelphia	26		1917	Cincinnati	21
1909	Philadelphia	40		1918	Cincinnati	12
19010	Philadelphia	28		1920	Cincinnati	21
				1921	Cincinnati	18

A. Seminick

1946	Philadelphia	14		B. Santiago		
1948	Philadelphia	22		1987	San Diego	32
1949	Philadelphia	12		1988	San Diego	12
1950	Philadelphia	15		1989	San Diego	20
1952	Cincinnati	13		1991	San Diego	14
				1992	San Diego	12
				1993	Florida	11

<u>Catcher's with 1,100 Total Changes</u>

Five times it happened. In 1997, Dan Wilson became the first and only backstop to record 1,100 total chances in the American League. In order to reach that total, a team must have plenty of strikeout pitchers.

<u>American League</u>				<u>National League</u>			
1997	D. Wilson	Seattle	1,129	1969	J. Edwards	Houston	1,221
2014	Y. Gomes	Cleveland	1,139	1996	M. Piazza	Los Angeles	1,135
2014	S. Perez	KC	1,118	1997	M. Piazza	Los Angeles	1,135
				2003	P. Lo Duca	Los Angeles	1,129
				2007	R. Martin	Los Angeles	1,164
				2008	R. Martin	Los Angeles	1,118
				2008	J. Kendall	Milwaukee	1,125
				2009	R. Martin	Los Angeles	1,133
				2014	M. Montero	Arizona	1,115
				2015	Y. Molina	St Louis	1,127
				2015	W. Ramos	Washington	1,109

<u>Catchers with 1,000 Put Outs in a Season</u>

Remember that most strikeouts are putouts by the catcher.

National League				American League			
1963	J. Edwards	Cincinnati	1,008	1997	D. Wilson	Seattle	1,051
1969	J. Edwards	Houston	1,135	2014	Y. Gomes	Cleveland	1,052
1996	M. Piazza	Los Angeles	1,056	2014	M. Zunino	Seattle	1,010
1997	M. Piazza	Los Angeles	1,045	2014	S. Perez	KC	1,037
1998	J. Kendall	Pittsburgh	1,015				
2003	P. Lo Duca	Los Angeles	1,014				
2004	M. Barrett	Chicago	1,035				
2007	R. Martin	Los Angeles	1,065				
2008	R. Martin	Los Angeles	1,042				
2008	J. Kendall	Milwaukee	1,025				
2009	R. Martin	Los Angeles	1,039				
2011	J. Buck	Florida	1,008				
2014	M. Montero	Arizona	1,037				
2014	J. Lucroy	Milwaukee	1,013				
2015	Y. Molina	St Louis	1,064				
2015	W. Ramos	Washington	1,026				

Catchers With Two Hundred Assists in a Season

This has not happened since 1915, which was the "Dead Ball Era" in baseball. Base running was the big offensive weapon and catchers who had a rifle arm were in demand.

American League				National League			
1909	G. Street	Washington	210	1909	B. Berger	Brooklyn	202
1911	O. Stanage	Detroit	212	1910	G. Gibson	Pittsburgh	203
				1915	F. Synder	St. Louis	204

Note the last catcher to record 100 or more assists in the American League was Jim Sundberg in 1977 with 103 for Texas.

The last catcher to record 100 or more assists in the National League was Michael Barrett in 1999 with 104 for Montreal.

61

Outfielders in Fielding Records

Outfielders Percentage Leaders

You would have to go back to the "Dead Ball Era" to find the record holder who is Amos Strunk. He did it five times while in the National League the record is three shared by two men, one who is that man Stan.

American League

A. Strunk

Year	Team	%	Errors
1912	Philadelphia	.990	3
1914	Philadelphia	.987	4
1917	Philadelphia	.986	5
1918	Boston	.988	3
1920	Chicago	.985	3

W. Judnich

Year	Team	%	Errors
1940	St. Louis	.989	4
1942	St. Louis	.991	3
1946	St. Louis	.995	2

G. Woodling

Year	Team	%	Errors
1952	New York	.996	1
1953	New York	.996	1
1955	Baltimore/ Cleveland	.995	1

J. Piersall

Year	Team	%	Errors
1956	Boston	.991	4
1961	Cleveland	.991	3
1962	Washington	.997	1

K. Berry

Year	Team	%	Errors
1969	Chicago	1.000	0
1972	California	1.000	0
1973	California	.997	1

National League

S. Musial					T. Gonzalez			
Years	**Team**	**%**	**Errors**		**Year**	**Team**	**%**	**Errors**
1949	St. Louis	.991	3		1962	Philadelphia	1.000	0
1954	St. Louis	.990	3		1964	Philadelphia	.996	1
1961	St. Louis	.994	1		1967	Philadelphia	.993	2

Outfielders Leading League in Errors Most Times

This undistinguished record belongs to hall of famer and three hundred hit man Lou Brock. He did it a total of seven times, five of them consecutively. In the American League, two men share the record at five, with hall of famer Reggie Jackson being one of them.

American League

B. Shotton				R. Jackson		
1912	St. Louis	25		1968	Oakland	12
1914	St. Louis	24		1970	Oakland	12
1915	St. Louis	23		1972	Oakland	9
1916	St. Louis	20		1975	Oakland	12
1918	Washington	18		1976	Baltimore	11

National League

M. Carey				L. Brock		
1918	Pittsburgh	17		1964	Chicago/	14
1921	Pittsburgh	20			St. Louis	
1924	Pittsburgh	16		1965	St. Louis	12
1925	Pittsburgh	20		1966	St. Louis	19
				1967	St. Louis	13
				1968	St. Louis	14
				1972	St. Louis	13
				1973	St. Louis	12

D. Parker			V. Guerrero		
1976	Pittsburgh	14	1997	Montreal	12
1977	Pittsburgh	15	1998	Montreal	17
1978	Pittsburgh	12	1999	Montreal	19
1979	Pittsburgh	15	2000	Montreal	10
			2001	Montreal	12

Outfielder with 500 or More Total Chances in a Season

Out of the sixteen times it happened, Richie Ashburn did it six times. Of the sixteen times, only half of them resulted in 500 or more putouts.

American League
1924	B. Jacobson	St. Louis	502
1948	D. DiMaggio	Boston	526
1953	J. Busby	Washington	503
1954	J. Busby	Washington	503
1977	C. Lemon	Chicago	536
1980	D. Murphy	Oakland	525

National League
1928	T. Douthit	St. Louis	566
1931	L. Waner	Pittsburgh	515
1951	R. Ashburn	Philadelphia	560
1953	R. Ashburn	Philadelphia	519
1954	R. Ashburn	Philadelphia	503
1956	R. Ashburn	Philadelphia	523
1957	R. Ashburn	Philadelphia	527
1958	R. Ashburn	Philadelphia	511
1979	O. Moreno	Pittsburgh	514
1999	A. Jones	Atlantic	515

Outfield with Five Hundred Put Outs in a Season

In 1928, Taylor Douthit was the first to gather in five hundred flies. He set the record when he snagged 547 of them. The only other National to do 500 or more putouts was Richie Ashburn, who did it four times. Richie is also the only outfielder to do it in consecutive years (1956-1957).

In 1948, Dom DiMaggio was the first junior circuit outfielder to have 500 plus putouts.

American League

1948	D. DiMaggio	Boston	503
1977	C. Lemon	Chicago	512
1980	D. Murphy	Oakland	507

National League

1928	T. Douthit	St. Louis	547
1949	R. Ashburn	Philadelphia	514
1951	R. Ashburn	Philadelphia	538
1956	R. Ashburn	Philadelphia	503
1957	R. Ashburn	Philadelphia	502

Outfielders Leading the League in Assists

The records are held by two hall of famers who belong to the 3000 hit club. It shows that they were not just one-dimensional players.

American League			National League		
C.Yastrzemski			R. Clemente		
1962	Boston	15	1958	Pittsburgh	22
1963	Boston	18	1960	Pittsburgh	19
1964	Boston	19	1961	Pittsburgh	27
1966	Boston	15	1966	Pittsburgh	17
1969	Boston	17	1967	Pittsburgh	17
1971	Boston	16			

1977   Boston 16

Post Season Trivia

Play Off For A Playoff

Ten times in the history of the game, there has been a playoff for post-season play. The first time this occurred was in 1946, when the St. Louis Cardinals finished in a flatfooted tie for the Pennant with the Brooklyn Dodgers. The Cardinals, in a two out of three, beat the Dodgers two games to none.

Just to clarify, the 1946 playoff was the first playoff in Major League history. There must be a clarification of the 1908 pennant race. This was the year that the Chicago Cubs and New York Giants had the tie game due to the Fred Merkle boner. Merkle failed to touch second base on the winning hit for the Giants. Merkle was declared out and the game was ruled a tie. Among the mass confusion on the field, the game was to be played over again at season end but only if it had any meaning on the final outcome of the Pennant. It did with the Cubs defeating the Giants four to two. This was not a playoff game; it was a replay of the Merkle game.

In the American League, the first playoff for a Pennant was in 1948, between the Cleveland Indians and the Boston Red Sox. Cleveland was victorious in a one game affair.

There were three other Pennant playoffs, all in the National League. In fact, all four National League playoffs involved the Dodgers.

Since the beginning of the LCS and Division play, there have been five other playoffs. Three of them involved Division Champions and two wild card positions.

American League

Pennant Best One of One		Winning Pitcher	Losing Pitcher
1948	Cleveland 8 Boston 3	G. Bearden	D. Galehouse
	At Boston		

Division Title Best One of One		Winning Pitcher	Losing Pitcher
1978	New York 5 Boston 4	R. Guidry	M. Torres
	At Boston		
1995	Seattle 9 California 1	R. Johnson	M. Langston
	At Seattle		

National League

Pennant Best Two of Three		Winning Pitcher	Losing Pitcher
1946	St. Louis 4 Brooklyn 2	H. Pollet	R. Branch
	At St. Louis		
	St. Louis 8 Brooklyn 4	M. Dickson	J. Hatten
	At Brooklyn		
1951	New York 3 Brooklyn	J. Hearn	R. Branca
	At Brooklyn		
	Brooklyn 10 New York 0	C. Labine	S. Jones
	At New York		
	New York 5 Brooklyn 4	L. Jansen	R. Branch
	At New York		
1959	Los Angles 3 Milwaukee 5	L. Sherry	C. Willey
	At Milwaukee		
	Los Angles 6 Milwaukee 5	S. Williams	B. Rush
	At LA		

| 1962 | San Fran 8 | Los Angeles 0 | B. Pierce | S. Koufax |
| At SF | | | | |

| | LA 8 | San Francisco 7 | S. Williams | B. Bolin |
| At LA | | | | |

| | San Fran 6 | Los Angeles 4 | D. Larsen | E. Roebuck |
| At LA | | | | |

Division Series

Down Two to Zero in Games and Win Series

In 1981, due to the extended strike that eluded one-third of the season, it was decided that the season would be played as two halves. The two east winners would as well as the two west winners. This created the first Division Playoff. In 1995, the Divisional Playoff became a permanent arrangement when the leagues were broken down into three divisions. Those winners, along with a wild card entrée (the best second place finisher), would play for the Pennant and World Series.

American League   National League

1995 Seattle defeats New York 3-2 1981 Los Angles defeats Houston 3-2

1999   Boston defeats Cleveland 3-2

2001   New York defeats Oakland 3-2

Division Series Player with Five or More Home Runs

The record is eight home runs shared by two American Leagues and one National Leaguer. There are thirteen altogether with five or more dingers.

American League

Juan Gonzalez	Jim Thome	Edgar Martinez	Bernie Williams
1996 Texas	1995 Cleveland	1995 Seattle	1995 New York
1999 Texas	1998 Cleveland	1997 Seattle	1996 New York
2001 Cleveland	1999 Cleveland	2000 Seattle	1999 New York
	2001 Cleveland	2001 Seattle	2002 New York

Paul O'Neill	Nomar Garciappra	Ken Griffey Jr	M. Ramirez
1995 New York	1998 Boston	1995 Seattle	1996 Cleveland
1997 New York	1999 Boston		1998 Cleveland
1998 New York			2003 Boston

D. Jeter
1997 New York
2002 New York
2003 New York

National League

Chipper Jones	Ken Caminiti	Vinny Castilla	Jim Edmunds
1995 Atlanta	1996 San Diego	1995 Colorado	2000 St. Louis
1996 Atlanta	1999 Houston	2001 Houston	2001 St. Louis
1997 Atlanta	2002 Atlanta		2002 St. Louis
2001 Atlanta			
2003 Atlanta			

Division Series Pitchers with Four Wins or More

The first Division Series was in 1981, when the long strike forced the majors into two halves winners. The first half winner would meet the second half winner. The survivor would face off for the LCS with the winner going on to the World Series.

The Divisional Series became a permanent fixture in 1995, when the leagues were set up into three divisions with a wild card team (the best second place team). They would then determine the final two combatants for the LCS. Since the Division Series has a short history, there are not that many pitchers who have amassed that many wins. Only four were able to obtain that number, but in time that should be easily reached.

Series Shown is Where There Are Wins

American League

D. Wells New York	4-1	A. Pettitte	4-3
1996 Baltimore	1-0	1997	0-2
1997 New York	1-0	1998	1-0
1998 New York	1-0	1999	1-0
2002 New York	0-1	2000	1-0
2003 New York	1-0	2001	0-1
		2003	1-0

National League

J. Smoltz	5-0	G. Maddux	5-3
1996 Atlanta	1-0	1995 Atlanta	1-0
1997 Atlanta	1-0	1996 Atlanta	1-0
1998 Atlanta	1-0	1997 Atlanta	1-0
1999 Atlanta	1-0	1998 Atlanta	1-0
2003 Atlanta	1-0	1999 Atlanta	0-1
		2000 Atlanta	0-1
		2002 Atlanta	1-0
		2003 Atlanta	0-1

Combined Leagues

D. Wells

1995 Cincinnati	1-0
1996 New York	1-0
1997 New York	1-0
1998 New York	1-0
2002 New York	0-1
2003 New York	1-0

LCS Lose First Two Games but Win Series

There has been six occasions that a team was down 2-0 in games and came back to win the Series. From 1969 through 1984, the LCS was a best three of five format. In 1985, it was changed to the best four of seven arrangements.

American League

| 1982 | Milwaukee defeats California | 3-2 |
| 1982 | Kansas City defeats Toronto | 4-3 |

National League

| 1984 | San Diego defeats Chicago | 3-2 |
| 1985 | St. Louis defeats Los Angeles | 4-2 |

LCS Winning Last Two Games on the Road

This scenario took place three times. The first time was a five game series; the other two were seven game encounters.

American League	National League
1985 Kansas City defeats Toronto 4-3	1980 Philadelphia defeats Houston 3-2
	1991 Atlanta defeats Pittsburgh 4-3

LCS has been down three to one in games that have won the series. This has happened three times. It was consecutive in the American League two times.

American League	National League
1985 Kansas City defeats Toronto 4-3	1996 Atlanta defeats St. Louis 4-3
1986 Boston defeats California 4-3	

LCS Players with Five or More Home Runs

In this series the record is nine, which is held by an American Leaguer. The National League record is eight. Some interesting names are on this list.

American League

George Brett	Manny Ramirez	Bernie Williams	Jim Thome
1976 KC	1995 Cleveland	1996 New York	1995 Cleveland
1978 KC	1997 Cleveland	1999 New York	1998 Cleveland
1980 KC	1998 Cleveland	2000 New York	
1985 KC	2002 Boston	2003 New York	

Reggie Jackson	Sal Bando	Derek Jeter	Graig Nettles
1971 Oakland	1971 Oakland	1996 New York	1976 New York
1975 Oakland	1973 Oakland	1999 New York	1978 New York
1978 New York	1974 Oakland	2000 New York	1980 New York
1982 California			1981 New York

National League

Steve Garvey	Gary Mathews	Ron Gant	Greg Luzinski
1974 Los Angeles	1983 Philadelphia	1991 Atlanta	1976 Philadelphia
1978 Los Angeles	1984 Chicago	1992 Atlanta	1977 Philadelphia
1981 Los Angeles	1996 St. Louis		1978 Philadelphia
1984 San Diego			1980 Philadelphia

Johnny Bench	Javy Lopez
1970 Cincinnati	1995 Atlanta
1972 Cincinnati	1996 Atlanta
1973 Cincinnati	1998 Atlanta
1976 Cincinnati	2001 Atlanta
1979 Cincinnati	

Combined Leagues

Darryl Strawberry	Dave Justice	John Olerud	Paul O'Neill
1986 New York NL	1991 Atlanta NL	1992 Toronto AL	1990 Cincinnati NL
1988 New York NL	1992 Atlanta NL	1999 New York NL	1996 New York AL
1996 New York AL	1998 Cleveland AL	2000 Seattle AL	1998 New York AL
1999 New York AL	2000 New York AL	2001 Seattle AL	2001 New York AL

LCS Pitchers with Five or More Wins (Series Shown is Where There Are Wins)

The LCS started in 1969, when the second expansion became a reality. Each league had twelve teams, making it feasible to have two divisions in each league. The winners of each division would meet for the LCS with the champion going on to the World Series. Only five pitchers have gathered five or more wins at this time.

American League

D. Stewart	A. Pettitte	J. Guzman
1988 Oakland 1-0	1996 New York 1-0	1991 Toronto 1-0
1989 Oakland 2-0	1999 New York 1-0	1992 Toronto 2-0
1990 Oakland 2-0	2000 New York 1-0	1993 Toronto 2-0
1992 Oakland 1-0	2001 New York 2-0	
1993 Toronto 2-0	2003 New York 1-0	

National League

J. Smoltz	T. Glavine
1991 Atlanta 2-0	1993 Atlanta 1-0
1992 Atlanta 2-0	1996 Atlanta 1-1
1996 Atlanta 2-0	1997 Atlanta 1-1
	1998 Atlanta 1-0
	2001 Atlanta 1-1

Seventh Game in Seven Game Series

The first World Series that went the distance was the 1909 encounter between Pittsburgh and Detroit. This was a series which each team won alternate games. In total there are thirty-seven World Series that went the distance, with the National League winning 22 times and the American League winning 15 times. The 1912 series was best of seven but there was a tie game which required and eighth game.

Since 1960, there have been 21 occasions that the Championship has been decided in one winner-take-all game.

American League Winners   (R)=Relief Pitcher

Year	Team	Score	Winning Pitcher	Losing Team	Losing Pitcher
1912	Boston	3-2	Wood (R)	New York	Mathewson (10 innings)
1926	Washington	4-3	Johnson (R)	New York	Bentley (12 innings)
1945	Detroit	9-3	Newhouser	Chicago	Borowy
1947	New York	5-2	Page (R)	Brooklyn	Gregg
1952	New York	4-2	Reynolds (R)	Brooklyn	Black
1956	New York	9-0	Kucks	Brooklyn	Newcomb
1958	New York	6-2	Turley (R)	Milwaukee	Burdette
1962	New York	1-0	Terry	San Francisco	Sanford
1968	Detroit	4-1	Lolich	St. Louis	Gibson
1972	Oakland	3-2	Hunter	Cincinnati	Borbon (R)
1973	Oakland	5-2	Holtzman	New York	Matlack
1985	Kansas City	11-0	Saberhagen	St. Louis	Tudor
1987	Minnesota	4-2	Viola	St. Louis	Magrane
1991	Minnesota	1-0	Morris	Atlanta	Pena (R) (10 innings)
2002	Anaheim	4-1	Lackey	San Francisco	Hernandez

National League Winners (R)= Relief Pitcher

Year	Team	Score	Winning Pitcher	Losing Team	Losing Pitcher
1909	Pittsburgh	8-0	Adams	Detroit	Donavan
1925	Pittsburgh	9-7	Kremer (R)	Washington	Johnson
1926	St. Louis	3-2	Haines	New York	Hoyt
1931	St. Louis	4-2	Grimes	Philadelphia	Earnshaw
1934	St. Louis	11-0	Dean	Detroit	Fluker
1940	Cincinnati	2-1	Derringer	Detroit	Newsome
1946	St. Louis	4-3	Brecheen (R)	Boston	Klinger (R)
1955	Brooklyn	2-0	Podres	New York	Byrne
1957	Milwaukee	5-0	Burdette	New York	Larsen
1960	Pittsburgh	10-9	Haddix (R)	New York	Terry (R)
1964	St. Louis	7-5	Gibson	New York	Stottlemyre
1965	Los Angeles	2-0	Koufax	Minnesota	Kaat
1967	St. Louis	7-2	Gibson	Boston	Lonborg
1971	Pittsburgh	2-1	Blass	Baltimore	Cuellar
1975	Cincinnati	4-3	Carroll (R)	Boston	Burton (R)
1979	Pittsburgh	4-1	Jackson (R)	Baltimore	McGregor
1982	St. Louis	6-3	Andujar	Milwaukee	McClure
1986	New York	8-5	McDowell (R)	Boston	Schiraldi (R)
1997	Florida	3-2	Powell (R)	Cleveland	Nagy (R)
2001	Arizona	3-2	Johnson (R)	New York	Rivera (R)
2011	St. Louis	6-2	Carpenter	Texas	Harrison
2014	San Francisco	3-2	Affeldt	Kansas City	Guthrie

World Series 1-0 Victories

Since the World Series started in 1905, there has been twenty-four 1-0 victories recorded. Six of them have been the clincher in the series. Two of those occurred in the seventh game with one being an extra inning affair.

American League

Date		AL	NL		WP	Hits	LP	Save	Game
9/5/18	A	Boston	Chicago	1-0	Ruth	6	Vaughn		1
10/11/20	H	Cleveland	Brooklyn	1-0	Mails	3	S. Smith		6
10/5/49	H	New York	Brooklyn	1-0	Reynolds	2	Newcomb		1
10/4/50	A	New York	Phila.	1-0	Raschi	2	Konstanty		1
10/6/59	A	Chicago	LA	1-0	Shaw	9	Koufax		5
10/16/62	A	New York	SF	1-0	Terry	4	Sanford		7*
10/8/66	H	Baltimore	LA	1-0	Bunker	6	O'Steen		3
10/9/66	H	Baltimore	LA	1-0	McNally	4	Drysdale		4*
10/18/86	A	Boston	New York	1-0	Hurst	5	Darling	Schiraldi	1
10/27/91	H	Minnesota	Atlanta	1-0	Morris	7	Pena		7#*
10/24/96	A	New York	Atlanta	1-0	Pettitte	5	Smoltz	Wetteland	5
10/26/05	A	Chicago	Houston	1-0	Garcia	5	Lidge	Jenks	4*

* Clinched Series
#Jack Morris CG 10 innings

National League

Date		NL	AL		WP	Hits	LP	Save	Game
10/13/05	H	New York	Phila.	1-0	McGinnity	5	Plank		4
10/12/06	A	Chicago	Chicago	1-0	Brown	2	Altrock		4
10/10/14	A	Boston	Phila.	1-0	James	2	Plank		2
10/13/21	A	New York	New York	1-0	Nehf	4	Hoyt		8*
10/12/23	A	New York	New York	1-0	Nehf	6	Jones		3
10/6/48	H	Boston	Cleveland	1-0	Sain	4	Feller		1
10/6/49	A	Brooklyn	New York	1-0	Roe	6	Raschi		2
10/9/56	H	Brooklyn	New York	1-0	Labine	7	Turley		6#
10/7/57	H	Milwaukee	New York	1-0	Burdette	7	Ford		5
10/5/63	H	LA	New York	1-0	Drysdale	3	Bouton		3
10/18/72	A	Cincinnati	Oakland	1-0	Billingham	3	Odom	Carroll	3
10/28/95	H	Atlanta	Cleveland	1-	Glavine	1	Poole	Wohlers	6

				0					*

* Clinched Series
# 10 innings - Both Clem Labine and Bob Turley pitched complete games

Zero to One World Series Clinches

Only six times has there been a series that ended with a 1-0 game. Only twice, it was a deciding seventh game. One was in 1962 when Willie McCovey hit a scorching line drive with two men in scoring position, in the ninth inning. The other occurred in 1991, with Jack Morris' ten-inning masterpiece.

1921 - New York National League 1-0 over New York 8 A. Nehf WP - W. Hoyt LP
1962 - New York American League 1-0 over San Francisco 7 R. Terry WP - J. Sanford LP
1966 - Baltimore 1-0 over Los Angeles 4 D. McNally WP - D. Drysdale LP
1991 - Minnesota 1-0 over Atlanta 7 J. Morris WP - A. Pena LP
1995 - Atlanta 1-0 over Cleveland 6 T. Glavine WP - J. Poole LP
2005 – Chicago American League over Houston F. Garcia WP – B. Lidge LP – B. Jenks (Save)

Consecutive One to Zero Games in a World Series

This has only happened twice in series history. In 1949, the adversaries swapped 1-0 victories. In 1966, the winner threw three consecutive shutouts with the last two being the one to zero showpieces.

10/5/49 - New York American League defeats Brooklyn National League 1-0 - A. Reynolds WP - D. Newcomb LP
10/6/49 - Brooklyn National League defeats New York American League 1-0 - P. Roe WP - V. Raschi LP
10/8/66 - Baltimore American League defeats Los Angles National League - W. Bunker WP - C. Osteen LP

10/9/66 - Baltimore American League defeats Los Angles National League - D. McNally WP - D. Drysdale

World Series Opponents Both Having One Hundred or More Wins

This has only happened seven times. Twice it was done in consecutive years.

1910
Philadelphia American League 102-48 Philadelphia won 4-1
Chicago National League 104-50

1912
Boston American League 105-47 Boston won 4-3
St. Louis National League 103-48

1931
Philadelphia American League 107-45 St. Louis won 4-3
St. Louis National League 101-53

1941
Philadelphia American League 101-53 New York won 4-1
Brooklyn National League 100-54

1942
New York American League 103-21 St. Louis won 4-1
St. Louis National League 106-48

1969
Baltimore American League 109-53
New York National League 100-62 New York won 4-1

1970
Baltimore American League 108-54
Cincinnati National League 102-60 Baltimore won 4-1

World Series Where Each Game Had an Alternate Winner

This has only happened three times with the latest happening in the 1997 series.

1909
1st Pittsburgh   National League (H) 4 - Detroit   American League 1
2nd Detroit   American League (A) 7 - Pittsburgh   National League 2
3rd Pittsburgh   National League   (A) 8 - Detroit   American League 6
4th Detroit   American League (H) 5 - Pittsburgh   National League 0
5th Pittsburgh   National League   (H) 8 - Detroit   American League 4
6th Detroit   American League (H) 5 - Pittsburgh   National League 4
7th Pittsburgh   National League   (A) 8 - Detroit   American League 0

1962
1st New York   American League (A) 6 - San Francisco National League 2
2nd San Francisco National League (H) 2 - New York American League   0
3rd New York   American League (H) 3 - San Francisco National League 2
4th San Francisco National League (A) 7 - New York American League   3
5th New York   American League (H) 5 - San Francisco National League 3
6th San Francisco National League (H) 5 - New York American League   2
7th New York   American League (A) 1 - San Francisco National League 0

1997
1st Florida National League (H) 7 - Cleveland American League 4
2nd Cleveland American League (A) 6 - Florida National League 1
3rd Florida National League (A) 14 - Cleveland American League 11
4th Cleveland American League (H) 10 - Florida National League 3
5th Florida National League (A) 8 - Cleveland American League 7
6th Cleveland American League (A) - 4 Florida National League 1
7th Florida National League (H) 3 - Cleveland American League 2

World Series Where the Home Team Won All Games

This scenario has occurred only twice. Both times the Minnesota Twins had the advantage of the schedule.

1987

1st Minnesota	American League	10	St. Louis National League		1
2nd Minnesota	American League	8	St. Louis National League		4
3rd St. Louis	National League	3	Minnesota American League		1
4th St. Louis	National League	7	Minnesota American League		2
5th St. Louis	National League	4	Minnesota American League		2
6th Minnesota	American League	11	St. Louis National League		5
7th Minnesota	American League	4	St. Louis National League		2

1991

1st Minnesota	American League	5	Atlanta National League		2
2nd Minnesota	American League	3	Atlanta National League		2
3rd Atlanta	National League	5	Minnesota American League		4
4th Atlanta	National League	3	Minnesota American League		2
5th Atlanta	National League	14	Minnesota American League		5
6th Minnesota	American League	4	Atlanta National League		3
7th Minnesota	American League	1	Atlanta National League		0

Teams Down Two to Zero in Games, Then Winning the World Series

The first time this occurred was in 1921, which was New York City's first subway series. After the Giants were down 2-0 in games, they came back in a torrent winning five of the next. The Babe Ruth-led Yankees could not stem the tide. There was no home field advantage since both teams claimed the polo grounds as their home site. This series was the last of the best five of nine formats. It would not have mattered if it were best of seven since the Giants had a 4-3 edge after seven games. Ten more times there have been series won when the eventual winner lost the first two games. Ironically, the last three occurrences happened when the home team lost the first two games.

1921 New York National League defeats New York American League 5-3

1955 Brooklyn National League defeats New York American League 4-3

1956 New York American League defeats Brooklyn National League 4-3

1958 New York American League defeats Milwaukee National League 4-3

1965 Los Angles National League defeats Minnesota American League 4-3

1971 Pittsburgh National League defeats Baltimore American League 4-3

1978 New York American League defeats Los Angeles National League 4-2

1981 Los Angeles National League defeats New York American League 4-2

*1985 Kansas City American League defeats St. Louis National League 4-3

*1986 New York National League defeats Boston American League 4-3

*1996 New York American League defeats Atlanta National League 4-2

*Winner lost its first two games at home.

Teams Down Three to One in Games, Then Winning the World Series

The first modern World Series took place in 1903 with the format being the best five out of nine. Boston was able to rally being down 3-1 in games with that extended format. There was good reason they were able to pull off victory. Pittsburgh's pitching staff was hampered when their top pitcher Sam Leever had to pitch with a sore arm. Ed Doheny had a break down and was lost for the Series. This left only Charles "Deacon" Phillippe and the only reliable starter. After three complete game victories, he melted down from arm fatigue, which was all Boston needed. Since that series, five other times a 3-1 deficit was overcome.

1903 Boston American League defeats Pittsburgh National League 6-3

1925 Pittsburgh National League defeats Washington 4-3

1958 New York American League defeats Milwaukee National League 4-3

1968 Detroit American League defeats St. Louis National League 4-3

1979 Pittsburgh National League defeats Baltimore American League 4-3

1985 Kansas City American League defeats St. Louis National League 4-3

Pitchers Who Have Won World Series Games for Both Leagues

Jack Coombs led Connie Mack's 1910 Philadelphia A's to the American League Pennant by winning 31 games. In the World Series against the Chicago Cubs, he won three more to aid the A's to the World Championship. Eventually, Coombs was released and picked up by the Brooklyn Dodgers. He pitched in with thirteen wins in 1916, which helped the Dodgers to win their first Pennant in modern times. In the Series against the World Champions Boston, he started and won the third game 4-3. It was the first World Series victory for Brooklyn. More significantly, Coombs became the first pitcher to win a World Series game for a team in both leagues.

	American League		National League	
1) Jack Coombs	Philadelphia	1910, 1911	Brooklyn	1916
2) Hank Borowy	New York	1943	Chicago	1945
3) Johnny Sain	New York	1953	Boston	1948

83

4) Don Larsen New York	1956, 1957, 1958	San Francisco	1962
5) Tommy John New York	1981	Los Angeles	1978
6) Bert Blyleven Minnesota	1987	Pittsburgh	1979
7) Rick Aguilera Minnesota	1991	New York	1986
8) Mike Stanton New York	2000	Atlanta	1991
9) Josh Beckett Boston	2007	Florida	2003
10) Curt Schilling Boston	2004, 2007	Arizona	2001
11) Ryan Madson KC	2015	Philadelphia	2008

Note: The years shown are the years each pitcher won a game in the Series.

Pitchers with Three Wins in One World Series

Since the World Series has been played, thirteen times a pitcher was victorious three times in one World Series. To erase any confusion, some Series had a best five of nine formats. This was so in the 1903 Series when both teams boasted in having a three game winner. The 1912 Series was one of three Series that had a tie game. Just a note for trivia buffs, that only three left-handers were three game winners. These were Harry Brecheen in 1946, Mickey Lolich in 1968, and more recently Randy Johnson in 2001.

American League

Year	Name	Team	Game Number	Opponent
1903	B. Dinneen	Boston	2,6,8	Pittsburgh
1910	J. Coombs	Philadelphia	2,3,5	Chicago
1912	J. Word	Boston	1,4,8	New York
1917	U. Faber	Chicago	2,5,6	New York

| 1920 | S. Coveleski | Cleveland | 1,4,7 | Brooklyn |
| 1968 | M. Lolich | Detroit | 2,5,7 | St. Louis |

National League

Year	Name	Team	Game Number	Opponent
1903	C. Phillippe	Pittsburgh	1,3,4	Boston
1905	C. Mathewson	New York	1,3,5	Philadelphia
1909	B. Adams	Pittsburgh	1,5,7	Detroit
1946	H. Brecheen	St. Louis	2,6,7	Boston
1957	L. Burdette	Milwaukee	2,5,7	New York
1967	B. Gibson	St. Louis	1,4,7	Boston
2001	R. Johnson	Arizona	2,6,7	New York

World Series Pitcher with Five or More Wins

This has been done thirteen times. Nine of the pitchers are American Leaguers with seven New York Yankees making the list. This shows how dominant the Yankees were down through the ages.

American League (Series shown are wins)

W. Ford (10)
1950 New York 1-0
1955 New York 2-0
1956 New York 1-1
1957 New York 1-1
1960 New York 2-0
1961 New York 2-0
1962 New York 1-0

R. Ruffing (7)
1932 New York 1-0
1937 New York 1-0
1938 New York 2-0
1939 New York 1-0
1941 New York 1-0
1942 New York 1-1

A. Reynolds (7)
1947 New York 1-0
1949 New York 1-0
1950 New York 1-0
1951 New York 1-1
1952 New York 2-1
1953 New York 1-0

L. Gomez (6)
1932 New York 1-0
1936 New York 2-0
1937 New York 2-0
1938 New York 1-0

C. Bender (6)
1905 Philadelphia 1-1
1910 Philadelphia 1-1
1911 Philadelphia 2-1
1913 Philadelphia 2-0

W. Hoyt (6)
1921 New York 2-1
1926 New York 1-1
1927 New York 1-0
1928 New York 2-0

H. Pennock (5)	V. Raschi (5)	C. Hunter (5)
1923 New York 2-0	1949 New York 1-1	1972 Oakland 2-0
1926 New York 2-0	1950 New York 1-0	1973 Oakland 1-0
1927 New York 1-0	1951 New York 1-1	1974 Oakland 1-0
	1952 New York 2-0	1975 New York 1-1

National League

B. Gibson (7)	M. Brown (5)	C. Mathewson (5)
1964 St. Louis 2-1	1906 Chicago 1-2	1905 New York 3-0
1967 St. Louis 3-0	1907 Chicago 1-0	1911 New York 1-2
1968 St. Louis 2-1	1908 Chicago 2-0	1913 New York 1-1
	1910 Chicago 1-2	

World Series Balk

The first World Series balk took place during the 1912 World Series. The dubious distinction in making this misplay belongs to Tom "Buck" O'Brien of the Boston Red Sox. The first National League balk occurred in the 1919 World Series with the culprit being a Cincinnati Red's pitcher and not a "Black Sox" Chicagoan. "Slim" Sallee made the blunder.

The twenties saw two more balks with the next being twenty-two years later in 1948. Only twice has there been more than one balk in a Series. Oddly, it happened in consecutive years (1987 and 1988). In 1987, two twin pitchers were responsible for the mishap while in 1988, both sides were guilty of balking.

American League

Year	Pitcher	Team	Game	Inning
1912	B. O'Brien	Boston	6	First
1948	B. Lemon	Cleveland	6	Second
1953	V. Raschi	New York	3	Fifth
1967	J. Wyatt	Boston	1	Ninth

1975	L. Tiant	Boston	1	Forth
1979	S. McGregor	Baltimore	3	First
1982	D. Sutton	Milwaukee	6	Forth
1983	S. Stewart	Baltimore	4	Sixth
1984	D. Petry	Detroit	2	Second
1987	L. Straker	Minnesota	3	Second
1987	K. Atherton	Minnesota	5	Seventh
1988	D. Stewart	Oakland	1	First
1996	D. Weathers	New York	4	Fifth

National League

1919	S. Sallee	Cincinnati	2	Sixth
1925	V. Aldridge	Pittsburgh	2	Third
1926	H. Bell	St. Louis	4	Fifth
1952	B. Loes	Brooklyn	6	Seventh
1965	R. Perranoski	Los Angeles	2	Eighth
1985	R. Horton	St. Louis	3	Seventh
1988	T. Leary	Los Angeles	3	Third
1989	J. Brantley	San Francisco	3	Fifth
1991	T. Glavine	Atlanta	2	Eighth
1995	S. Avery	Atlanta	4	Sixth

Players Who Hit World Series Homers for Both Leagues

The first to accomplish this was Enos Slaughter. Playing for the St. Louis Cardinals in the 1946 Series, "Country" smacked the only Red Bird four Bagger in the second inning of the third game, off of Boston Red Sox "Tex" Hughson. His next Series appearance came in 1956, while playing for the New York Yankees. Enos in the sixth inning of the third game hit a three run homer off Brooklyn's Roger Craig. This was the impetus to spur the Yankees on towards victory. Also significantly, it was the first time a player hit a Series home run while playing in both leagues. Since Slaughter's feat, six others performed the deed.

The last man to achieve the feat is Matt Williams. He was the distinction of hitting a home run for three different teams.

Enos Slaughter	St. Louis	National League	1946
	New York	American League	1956
Bill Skowron	New York	American League	
1955,1956,1958,1960,1961			
	Los Angeles	National League	1963
Roger Maris	New York	American League	
1960,1961,1962,1964			
	St. Louis	National League	1967
Reggie Smith	Boston	American League	1967
	Los Angeles	National League	1977,1978
Frank Robinson	Cincinnati	National League	1961
	Baltimore	American League	
1966,1969,1970,1971			
Kirk Gibson	Detroit	American League	1984
	Los Angeles	National League	1988
Matt Williams	San Francisco	National League	1989
	Cleveland	American League	1997
	Arizona	National League	2001

Award Winning Trivia

Awards That Have had a Tie Vote

Four times in the games' history has there been tie votes in the yearly awards. The MVP had a tie vote in the National League for 1979. The American League had a tie vote for the Cy Young award in 1969. Twice the ROY had tie votes, once in the National League for 1976 and in the American League for 1979.

MVP 1979 National League
Willie Stargell Pittsburgh
Keith Hernandez St. Louis

Cy Young 1969 American League
Denny McLain Detroit
Mike Cuellar Baltimore

ROY 1976 National League
Butch Metzger San Diego
Pat Zachry Cincinnati

ROY 1979 American League
Alfredo Griffin Toronto
John Castino Minnesota

Only Players To Win Two Different Awards Unanimously

Only three players have done it. Two were ROY and MVP, and one pitcher took MVP and Cy Young.

Frank Robinson	Cincinnati ROY 1956 Baltimore MVP 1966
Orlando Cepeda	San Francisco ROY 1958 St. Louis MVP 1967
Denny McLain	Detroit MVP 1968 Detroit Cy Young 1968
Albert Pujols	St. Louis ROY 2001 St. Louis ROY 2009

Mike Trout   Los Angeles Angels ROY 2012
                    Los Angeles Angels MVP 2014

Teams with Cy Young and ROY Winners

This combination of award winners is even skimpier than the other combos. Five times this has happened with Fernando Valenzuela being the only pitcher to take both the same year.

American League			National League		
1983 Chicago	CY	L. Hoyt	1965 Los Angles	CY	S. Koufax
	ROY	R. Kittle		ROY	J. Lefebvre
1994 KC	CY	D. Cone	1976 San Diego	CY	R. Jones
	ROY	B. Hamelin		ROY	B. Metzger
2015 Houston	CY	D. Keuchel	1981 Los Angeles	CY	F. Valenzuela
	ROY	C. Correa		ROY	F. Valenzuela
			2015 Chicago	CY	J. Arrieta
				ROY	K. Bryant

Teams with The MVP and ROY in The Same Year

This has been rarer than the MVP and Cy Young combination. Out of the eleven times this combo has taken place, rookies have taken both awards.

American League			National League		
1951 New York	MVP	Y. Berra	1949 Brooklyn	MVP	J. Robinson
	ROY	G. McDougal		ROY	D. Newcomb
1952 Philadelphia	MVP	B. Schantz	1953 Brooklyn	MVP	R. Campanella
	ROY	H. Byrd		ROY	J. Gillian
1954 New York	MVP	Y. Berra	1976 Cincinnati	MVP	J. Morgan
	ROY	B. Grim		ROY	P. Zachry

1957	New York	MVP	M. Mantle
		ROY	T. Kubek

1962	New York	MVP	M. Mantle
		ROY	T. Tresh

1975	Boston	MVP	F. Lynn
		ROY	F. Lynn

1988	Oakland	MVP	J. Canseco
		ROY	W. Weiss

2001	Seattle	MVP	I. Suzuki
		Roy	I. Suzuki

Teams with The MVP and Cy Young Winners in The Same Year

This has happened twenty-three times since the Cy Young award was started in 1956. Pitchers have captured both prizes nine times, three being relief pitchers.

American League

1959 Chicago	MVP	N. Fox
	CY	E. Wynn

1961 New York	MVP	R. Maris
	CY	W. Ford

1967 Boston	MVP	C. Yastrzemski
	CY	J. Lonborg

1968 Detroit	MVP	D. McLain
	CY	D. McLain

1971 Oakland	MVP	V. Blue
	CY	V. Blue

National League

1956 Brooklyn	MVP	D. Newcomb
	CY	D. Newcomb

1960 Pittsburgh	MVP	D. Groat
	CY	V. Law

1963 Los Angeles	MVP	S. Koufax
	CY	S. Koufax

1968 St. Louis	MVP	B. Gibson
	CY	B. Gibson

1974 Los Angeles	MVP	S. Garvey
	CY	M. Marshall

1981 Milwaukee	MVP	R. Finger	1980 Philadelphia	MVP	M. Schmidt
	CY	R. Finger		CY	S. Carlton
1982 Milwaukee	MVP	R. Yount	1984 Chicago	MVP	R. Sandberg
	CY	P. Vuckovich		CY	R. Sutcliffe
1984 Detroit	MVP	W. Hernandez	1988 Los Angeles	MVP	K. Gibson
	CY	W. Hernandez		CY	O. Hershiser
1986 Boston	MVP	R. Clemens	1990 Pittsburgh	MVP	B. Bonds
	CY	R. Clemens		CY	D. Drabek
1990 Oakland	MVP	R. Hernandez	1991 Atlanta	MVP	T. Pendleton
	CY	B. Welch		CY	T. Glavine
1993 Chicago	MVP	F. Thomas	2005 St Louis	MVP	A. Pujols
	CY	J. McDowell		CY	C. Carpenter
2002 Oakland	MVP	M. Tejada	2014 Los Angeles	MVP	C. Kershaw
	CY	B. Zito		CY	C. Kershaw
2006 Minnesota	MVP	J. Mauer			
	CY	J. Santana			
2011 Detroit	MVP	J. Verlander			
	CY	J. Verlander			
2013 Detroit	MVP	M. Cabrera			
	CY	M. Scherzer			

Pitchers Who Won MVP and Cy Young Same Year

Before 1956, there was no pitching award for excellence. Pitchers had to compete with every day players who had the advantage in the voting. Out of forty-eight awards, a pitcher has only won ten times. When the Cy Young award was initiated, pitchers were still eligible for the MVP.

American League			National League		
1968	D. McLain	Detroit	1956	D. Newcomb	Brooklyn
1971	V. Blue	Oakland	1963	S. Koufax	Los Angeles
1981	R. Fingers	Milwaukee	1968	B. Gibson	St. Louis
1984	W. Hernandez	Detroit	2014	C. Kershaw	Los Angeles
1986	R. Clemens	Boston			
1992	D. Eckersley	Oakland			
2011	J. Verlander	Detroit			

Prior to Cy Young Award, Pitchers Who Were MVP Winners

American League			National League		
1931	L. Grove	Philadelphia	1933	C. Hubbell	New York
1943	S. Chandler	New York	1934	D. Dean	St. Louis
1944	H. Newhouser	Detroit	1936	C. Hubbell	New York
1945	H. Newhouser	Detroit	1939	B. Walters	Cincinnati
1952	B. Shantz	Philadelphia	1942	M. Cooper	St. Louis
			1950	J. Konstanty	Philadelphia

Players with Three Or More MVP Awards

Only seven players can fit into this category. Barry Bonds has monopolized the award in the National League. Since the new century, he has double the amount of the other six. Bonds has the distinction of being the only player to win consecutive awards while playing for two different teams.

American League			National League		
J. Foxx	Philadelphia	1932	S. Musial	St. Louis	1943
J. Foxx	Philadelphia	1933	S. Musial	St. Louis	1946
J. Foxx	Boston	1938	S. Musial	St. Louis	1948

J. Dimaggio	New York	1939	R. Campanella	Brooklyn	1951
J. Dimaggio	New York	1941	R. Campanella	Brooklyn	1953
J. Dimaggio	New York	1947	R. Campanella	Brooklyn	1955
Y. Berra	New York	1951	B. Bonds	Pittsburgh	1990
Y. Berra	New York	1954	B. Bonds	Pittsburgh	1992
Y. Berra	New York	1955	B. Bonds	San Francisco	1993
			B. Bonds	San Francisco	2001
M. Mantle	New York	1956	B. Bonds	San Francisco	2002
M. Mantle	New York	1957	B. Bonds	San Francisco	2003
M. Mantle	New York	1962	B. Bonds	San Francisco	2004
			A. Pujols	St. Louis	2005
			A. Pujols	St. Louis	2008
			A. Pujols	St. Louis	2009

Only Teams with an MVP at Every Position

The St. Louis Cardinals and the Yankees are the only teams that can boast about this distinction.

St. Louis Cardinals

First Base	Orlando Cepeda	1967
Second Base	Frankie Frisch	1931
Short Stop	Marty Marion	1944
Third Base	Ken Boyer	1964
Catcher	Bob O'Farrell	1926
Outfield	Stan Musial	1943, 1948
Outfield	Joe Medwick	1937
Outfield	Willie McGee	1985
Pitcher	Dizzy Dean	1937

The Cardinals have had seventeen total MVP winners. Fourteen of them are from the BWAA, and three are league award recipients. Also, note that there are several positions that have multiple selections.

New York Yankees

First Base	Lou Gehrig	1936
Second Base	Joe Gordon	1942
Short Stop	Phil Rizzuto	1950
Third Base	Alex Rodriguez	2005, 2007
Catcher	Yogi Berra	1951, 1954, 1955
Outfield	Joe DiMaggio	1939, 1941, 1947
Outfield	Mickey Mantle	1956, 1957, 1962
Outfield	Roger Maris	1960, 1961
Pitcher	Spud Chandler	1943

The Yankees have had twenty-two total MVP winners. Twenty of them are from the BWAA, and two are league award recipients. Also, note that there are several positions that have multiple selections.

Players Winning The MVP While Playing Two Different Positions

This has been done only three times in the game's history. It shows the versatility of the player while maintaining their high level of play.

American League	National League		
1935 H. Greenberg Detroit 1B	1943 S. Musial	St. Louis	OF
1940 H. Greenberg Detroit OF	1946 S. Musial	St. Louis	1B
	1948 S. Musial	St. Louis	OF
	1982 R. Yount	Milwaukee	SS
	1989 R. Yount	Milwaukee	OF

Players Winning MVP While Playing for Two Different Teams

So far, only three players have accomplished this. Frank Robinson is the only one to win in both leagues.

American League

J. Foxx Philadelphia 1932, 1933
              Boston   1938

A. Rodriguez Texas   2003
              New York   2005, 2007

National League

B. Bonds Pittsburgh   1990, 1992
              San Francisco   1993, 2001,
                                    2002, 2003, 2004

Both Leagues

F. Robinson Cincinnati National League   1961
                Baltimore American League 1966

Unanimous MVP Selections

Hank Greenberg became the first to do it. It took almost two decades before it occurred again. The National League did not see a unanimous selection until 1967, thirty-six years after the award was initiated. Denny McLain is the only pitcher to win the award unanimously.

American League

1935	Hank Greenberg	Detroit
1953	Al Rosen	Cleveland
1956	Mickey Mantle	New York
1966	Frank Robinson	Baltimore
1968	Denny McLain	Detroit
1973	Reggie Jackson	Oakland
1988	Jose Canseco	Oakland
1993	Frank Thomas	Chicago
2014	Mike Trout	Los Angeles

National League

1967	Orlando Cepeda	St. Louis
1980	Mike Schmidt	Philadelphia
1994	Jeff Bagwell	Houston
1996	Ken Caminiti	San Diego
2002	Barry Bonds	San Francisco
2009	Albert Pujols	St. Louis
2015	Bryce Harper	Washington

Pitchers Who Were the First To Win MVP Righty And Lefty

The following list shows those who fit the category.

American League

National League

First Left Hander
1931 "Lefty" Grove Philadelphia

First Left Hander
1933 Carl Hubbell   New York

First Right Hander
1943 "Spud" Chandler New York

First Right Hander
1934 "Dizzy" Dean St. Louis

Teams With The Most Players Winning The MVP While Playing For The Team

Only two teams can lay claim to this. The New York Yankees and the Cincinnati Reds.

New York Yankees	1963	Cincinnati Reds	1977
Yogi Berra	1951, 1954, 1955	Johnny Bench	1970, 1972
Mickey Mantel	1956, 1957, 1962	Pete Rose	1973
Roger Maris	1960, 1961	Joe Morgan	1975, 1976
Elsten Howard	1963	George Foster	1977

Switch Hitters Who Won MVP

It seems that many baseball fans are amazed that switch-hitting is a highly regarded art. Little do they realize is that switch-hitting has not been that highly esteemed when the MVP (BWAA) award has been given. Out of one hundred and forty-four awards given, a switch hitter has been honored only twelve times, with one honoree winning it three times. That was the late Mickey Mantle.

American League

National League

M. Mantle	New York	1956, 1957, 1962	F. Frisc	St. Louis	1931
V. Blue	Oakland	1971	M. Wills	Los Angeles	1962
			P. Rose	Cincinnati	1973

W. McGee   St. Louis   1985
T. Pendleton Atlanta   1991
K. Caminiti   San Diego   1996
C. Jones   Atlanta   1999
J. Rollins   Philadelphia 2007

Triple Crown Hitters and MVP in the Same Year

You would think a player who wins the batting Triple Crown would be the odds on favorite to be the MVP. Since the MVP award has been in existence, only six of the ten Triple Crown winners during that period have been selected MVP. Lou Gehrig, Ted Williams twice, and Chuck Klein have been snubbed.

American League

Year	Name	Team	Batting Average	Home Runs	Runs Batted In
1933	Jimmy Foxx	Philadelphia	.356	48	163
1956	Mickey Mantle	New York	.353	52	130
1966	Frank Robinson	Baltimore	.316	49	122
1967	Carl Yastrzemski	Boston	.326	44	121
2012	Miguel Cabrera	Detroit	.330	44	139

National League

1925	Roger Hornsby	St. Louis	.403	39	143
1937	Joe Medwick	St. Louis	.374	31	154

Cy Young winners Who Were First

These four pitchers have been the first in Cy Young Award history.

American League

National League

First Right Hander
1958   Bob Turley   New York

First Right Hander
1956   Don Newcomb Brooklyn

First Left Hander			First Left Hander		
1961	Whitey Ford	New York	1957	Warren Spahn	Milwaukee

Teams with The Most Pitchers Who Won the Cy Young Award While Pitching for The Team

Only one team can claim the laurels and that is the Atlanta Braves. The great trio of Maddux, Glavine and Smoltz took six awards while pitching from 1996 to 2002.

Greg Maddux 1993, 1994, 1995

Tom Glavine 1991, 1998

John Smoltz 1996

Pitcher Who Won the CY Young Award Unanimously

Up to 1967, there was only one award given between the two leagues. Because of Sandy Koufax's domination of the award, it was decided to give separate awards to each league. Koufax was completely masterful during the years he won it. He was cited three times and unanimously awarded each year. Koufax was the first to win it in consecutive years. Only Greg Maddux and Pedro Martinez duplicated Sandy's unanimous consecutive awards.

American League		National League	
1968 Denny McLain	Detroit	1963 Sandy Koufax	Los Angeles
1978 Ron Guidy	New York	1965 Sandy Koufax	Los Angeles
1986 Roger Clemens	Boston	1966 Sandy Koufax	Los Angeles
1998 Roger Clemens	Toronto	1968 Bob Gibson	St. Louis
1999 Pedro Martinez	Boston	1972 Steve Carlton	Philadelphia
2000 Pedro Martinez	Boston	1984 Rick Sutcliffe	Chicago
2004 Johan Santana	Minnesota	1985 Dwight Gooden	New York
2006 Johan Santana	Minnesota	1988 Orel Hershiser	Los Angeles

99

2011 Justin Verlander	Detroit	1994 Greg Maddux	Atlanta
		1995 Greg Maddux	Atlanta
		2002 Randy Johnson	Arizona
		2007 Jake Peavy	San Diego
		2010 Roy Halladay	Philadelphia
		2014 Clayton Kershaw	Los Angeles

Teams with The Most Players Winning ROY While Playing for The Team

In 1996, the Los Angeles Dodgers could boast that they are the only team that has five homegrown products in their line up. Who came close? Why, the Dodgers themselves.

Los Angeles Dodgers	1982
Rick Sutcliffe	1979
Steve Howe	1980
Fernando Valenzuela	1981
Steve Sax	1982

Los Angeles Dodgers	1996
Eric Karros	1992
Mike Piazza	1993
Raul Mondesi	1994
Hideo Nomo	1995
Todd Hollandsworth	1996

Unanimous ROY Selections

Out of the fifteen times a ROY was selected unanimously, two teams can lay claim of having consecutive years of unanimous choices. The San Francisco Giants did this in 1958 and 1959 with Cepeda and McCovey. The Los Angeles Dodgers duplicated that in 1993 and 1994 with Piazza and Mondesi.

100

American League

1972	C. Fisk	Boston	Catcher
1987	M. McGwire	Oakland	First Base
1990	S. Alomar	Cleveland	Outfield
1993	T. Salmon	California	Outfield
1996	D. Jeter	New York	Short Stop
1997	N. Garciaparra	Boston	Short Stop
2008	E. Longoria	Tampa Bay	Third Base
2012	M. Trout	Los Angeles	Outfield
2014	J. Abreu	Chicago	Outfield

National League

1956	F. Robinson	Cincinnati	Outfield
1958	O. Cepeda	San Francisco	First Base
1959	W. McCovey	San Francisco	First Base
1985	V. Coleman	St. Louis	Outfield
1987	B. Santiago	San Diego	Catcher
1993	M. Piazza	Los Angeles	Catcher
1994	R. Mondesi	Los Angeles	Outfield
1997	S. Rolen	Philadelphia	Third Base
2001	A. Pujols	St. Louis	Outfield
2011	C. Kimbrel	Atlanta	Pitcher
2015	K. Bryant	Chicago	Third Base

Switch Hitters Winning ROY

Only eleven times since 1947, has a switch hitter taken home the honors. Only one eventually became a Hall of Famer.

American League

1962	T. Tresh	New York	Outfield-Short Stop
1977	E. Murray	Baltimore	DH-First Base
1979	A. Griffin	Toronto	Shortstop
1988	W. Weiss	Oakland	Shortstop
1992	P. Listach	Milwaukee	Shortstop

| 1999 | C. Beltran | KC | Outfield |

National League

1953	J. Gilliam	Brooklyn	Second Base
1963	P. Rose	Cincinnati	Second Base
1965	J. Lefebvre	Los Angeles	Second Base
1985	V. Coleman	St. Louis	Outfield
2000	R. Furcal	Atlanta	Shortstop

Teams That Have a Gold Glove Winner At Each Position

Surprisingly, there are only four teams that can make that statement. The St. Louis Cardinals joined the list as the only National League team in 2001. Fernando Vina won his first Gold Glove at second base filling the only empty spot the Red Birds had vacant. When outfielders are chosen, it is not by their outfield position. The three highest vote getters are selected.

American League

Boston Red Sox

First Base	G. Scott	(3)
Second Base	D. Griffin	(1)
Shortstop	R. Burleson	(1)
Third Base	F. Malzone	(3)
Catcher	C. Fisk	(1)
Outfield	D. Evans	(8)
Outfield	C. Yastrzemski	(3)
Outfield	F. Lynn	(3)
Pitcher	M. Boddicker	(1)

Chicago White Sox

First Base	J. Spencer	(1)
Second Base	N. Fox	(3)
Shortstop	L. Aparicio	(7)
Third Base	R. Ventura	(4)
Catcher	S. Collar	(3)
Outfield	M. Minoso	(3)
Outfield	J. Landis	(4)
Outfield	T. Agee	(1)
Pitcher	J. Kaat	(2)

Washington/Minnesota

First Base	V. Power	(2)
Second Base	C. Knoblauch	
Shortstop	Z. Versalles	(2)
Third Base	G. Gaetti	(4)
Catcher	E. Battey	(3)

Outfield	T. Oliva	(1)
Outfield	K. Puckett	(6)
Outfield	T. Hunter	(1)
Pitcher	J. Kaat	(12)

National League

St. Louis Cardinals

First Base	B. White	(6)
Second Base	F. Vina	(2)
Short Base	O. Smith	(11)
Third Base	C. Boyer	(5)
Catcher	T. Pagnozzi	(3)
Outfield	W. McGee	(2)
Outfield	J. Edmonds	(2)
Outfield	C. Flood	(7)
Pitcher	B. Gibson	(9)

Teams with Four Gold Glove Winners The Same Year

In The American League, it happened six times. The Baltimore Orioles can boast for five of the six, with three coming in consecutive years (1973-1975). The National League has nine teams doing it, with The Cincinnati Reds owning four of the nine. The Reds did theirs in consecutive years (1974-1977).

American League

1960 Chicago	1969 Baltimore	1971 Baltimore
Second Base N. Fox	Second Base D. Johnson	Second Base D. Johnson
Shortstop L. Aparicio	Third Base B. Robinson	Third Base B. Robinson
Outfield M. Minoso	Shortstop M. Belanger	Shortstop M. Belanger
Outfield J. Landis	Outfield P. Blair	Outfield P. Blair

1973 Baltimore	1974 Baltimore	1975 Baltimore
Second Base B. Grich	Second Base B. Grich	Second Base B. Grich
Third Base B. Robinson	Third Base B. Robinson	Third Base B. Robinson
Shortstop M. Belanger	Shortstop M. Belanger	Shortstop M. Belanger
Outfield P. Blair	Outfield P. Blair	Outfield P. Blair

National League

1974 Cincinnati	1975 Cincinnati	1976 Cincinnati
Catcher J. Bench	Catcher J. Bench	Catcher J. Bench
Second Base J. Morgan	Second Base J. Morgan	Second Base J. Morgan
Shortstop D. Concepcion	Shortstop D. Concepcion	Shortstop D. Concepcion
Outfield C. Geronimo	Outfield C. Geronimo	Outfield C. Geronimo

1977 Cincinnati	1978 Philadelphia	1979 Philadelphia
Catcher J. Bench	Catcher B. Boone	Catcher B. Boone
Second Base J. Morgan	Third Base M. Schmidt	Second Base M. Trillo
Shortstop D. Concepcion	Shortstop L. Bowa	Third Base M. Schmidt
Outfield C. Geronimo	Outfield G. Maddox	Outfield G. Maddox

1981 Philadelphia	1993 San Francisco	2002 St. Louis
Pitcher S. Carlton	Catcher K. Manwaring	Second Base F. Vina
Second Base M. Trillo	Second Base R. Thompson	Shortstop E. Renteria
Third Base M. Schmit	Third Base M. Williams	Third Base S. Rolen*
Outfield G. Maddox	Outfield B. Bonds	Outfield J. Edmonds

*Rolen also with Philadelphia

Gold Glove Winners Leading the League in Errors the Same Year

Sometimes you wonder how they select the Gold Glovers when a large number led the league in errors. You can name several at many positions. You can also make up a team with them.

Position	Name	Year	Team	Errors
First Base	Jeff Bagwell	1994	Houston	9
Second Base	Bill Mazerowski	1993	Pittsburgh	23
Shortstop	Zoilo Versalles	1965	Minnesota	39

Third Base	Frank Malzone	1958	Boston	27
Catcher	Thurman Munson	1974	New York	22
Outfielder	Kenny Lofton	1993	Cleveland	9
Outfielder	Tommy Agee	1970	New York	13
Outfielder	Dave Parker	1977	Pittsburgh	15
Pitcher (L)	Jim Kaat	1969	Minnesota	8
Pitcher (R)	Greg Maddox	1993	Atlanta	7

*Please note that Jim Kaat in 1969 had a .826 fielding average.

Three or More Hall of Fame Pitchers in the Same Rotation with at Least Ten Starts

It is a blessing for a team to have one pitcher that will eventually be a Hall of Famer on a staff. When two starters make it to Cooperstown, then you can say they are doubly blessed. When three make it to enshrinement, then that team was divinely endowed. This was shown by the Philadelphia A's from 1903 to 1907, and The Cleveland Indians with six consecutive years from 1949 thru 1954. Ironically, both teams won only one pennant each. They both were blown out in their only World Series appearance. One quick note about the 1954 Indians is that they did have a fourth Hall of Famer on the staff in Hal Newhouser. Prince Hal only made one start. He was primarily a relief pitcher going seven to two that year.

American League

	G.S.			G.S.			G.S.
1903 Philadelphia		**1904 Philadelphia**			**1905 Philadelphia**		
E. Plank 23-16	40	E. Plank 26-17	43	R. Waddell 26-11	34		
R. Waddell 22-16	38	R. Waddell 16-17	43	E. Plank 25-12	41		
C. Bender 17-15	33	C. Bender 10-11	20	C. Bender 16-11	23		
1906 Philadelphia		**1907 Philadelphia**			**1914 Philadelphia**		
E. Plank 19-5	25	E. Plank 24-16	40	C. Bender 17-3	23		
R. Waddell 16-16	34	R. Waddell 19-13	33	E. Plank 15-7	23		
C. Bender 15-10	27	C. Bender 16-6	24	H. Pennock 11-4	14		

105

1919 Boston			1931 New York			1932 New York		
H. Pennock	16-8	28	L. Gomez	21-9	26	L. Gomez	24-7	31
B. Ruth	8-5	15	R. Ruffing	16-14	30	R. Ruffing	18-7	29
W. Hoyt	4-6	11	H. Pennock	11-6	25	H. Pennock	9-5	21

1949 Cleveland			1950 Cleveland			1951 Cleveland		
B. Lemon	22-10	33	B. Lemon	23-11	37	B. Feller	22-8	32
B. Feller	15-14	28	E. Wynn	18-8	28	E. Wynn	20-13	34
E. Wynn	11-7	23	B. Feller	16-11	34	R. Lemon	17-14	34

1952 Cleveland			1953 Cleveland			1954 Cleveland		
E. Wynn	21-22	33	B. Lemon	21-14	36	B. Lemon	23-7	33
B. Lemon	22-11	36	E. Wynn	17-12	34	E. Wynn	23-11	36
B. Feller	9-13	30	B. Feller	10-7	25	B. Feller	13-3	19

National League

1916 Philadelphia			1917 Philadelphia			1933 St. Louis		
G. Alexander	33-12	45	G. Alexander	30-13	44	D. Dean	20-18	34
E. Rixey	22-10	33	E. Rixey	16-21	36	J. Haines	9-6	10
C. Bender	7-7	13	C. Bender	8-2	10	D. Vance	6-2	11

1966 Los Angeles		
S. Koufax	27-9	41
D. Drysdale	13-16	40
D. Sutton	12-12	35

Rookie Trivia

Rookies Leading The League in Batting Average

Has only happened twice in the game's history. Both times it was done in the American League.

American League
| 1964 Tony Olivia | Minnesota | .322 |
| 2001 Ichiro Suzuki | Seattle | .350 |

National League
Never accomplished

Rookie Thirty Home Run Hitters

Once a rarity, it is now becoming more common. Before 1960, only eight rookies managed to hit the mark. Since 1960, eighteen yearlings have added their names with Jose Abreu being the last in 2014.

American League

Name	Team	Year	Number
H. Trosky	Cleveland	1934	35
R. York	Detroit	1937	35
T. Williams	Boston	1939	31
A. Rosen	Cleveland	1950	37
W. Dropo	Boston	1950	34
B. Allison	Washington	1959	30
J. Hall	Minnesota	1963	33
T. Oliva	Minnesota	1964	32
R. Kittle	Chicago	1983	35
J. Conseco	Oakland	1986	33
P. Incaviglia	Texas	1986	30
M. McGwire	Oakland	1987	49

M. Nokes	Detroit	1987	32
T. Salmon	California	1993	31
N. Garciaparra	Boston	1997	30
M. Trout	Los Angeles	2012	30
J. Abreu	Chicago	2014	36

National League

W. Berger	Boston	1930	38
F. Robinson	Cincinnati	1956	38
J. Hart	San Francisco	1964	31
E. Williams	Atlanta	1971	33
W. Montanez	Philadelphia	1971	30
M. Piazza	Los Angeles	1993	35
A. Pujols	St. Louis	2001	37
R. Braun	Milwaukee	2007	34
C. Young	Arizona	2007	32

Rookies with .300 Batting Average, Thirty Homers and One Hundred RBI"S

When adding batting average to homers and RBI's we see the number of names sharing down to seven. Piazza and Pujols are names that are coated with greatness.

American League

Name	Team	Year	Batting	Home Runs	RBI
H. Trosky	Cleveland	1934	.330	35	142
R. York	Detroit	1937	.307	35	103
T. Williams	Boston	1934	.327	31	145
W. Dropo	Boston	1950	.322	34	144
J. Abreu	Chicago	2014	.317	36	107

National League

W. Berger	Boston	1930	.310	38	119
M. Piazza	Los Angles	1933	.318	35	112
A. Pujols	St. Louis	2001	.329	37	130

Rookie One Hundred RBI Hitters

This seems to be a long list of thirty-seven. However, when you consider how long the game has been played, since 1960 only eight have joined the list, which shows that first year men are having difficulty hitting the century mark in ribbies. The roll call is loaded with faded names that had their short stay in the sun. Cleveland has the lead with rookies hitting one hundred RBI's at six. When looking at the list, Cleveland has managed to have a pair of rookies break barrier in the same year. This was done twice in 1938 and 1950. The Red Sox duplicated the feat in 1975.

American League

Name	Team	Year	Total
A. Simmons	Philadelphia	1924	102
T. Lazzeri	New York	1926	114
D. Alexander	Detroit	1929	137
S. Jolley	Chicago	1930	114
J. Vosmik	Cleveland	1931	117
H. Trosky	Cleveland	1934	142
E. Bonura	Chicago	1934	110
R. Pepper	St. Louis	1934	101
J. DiMaggio	New York	1936	125
R. York	Detroit	1937	103
K. Keltner	Cleveland	1938	113
J. Heath	Cleveland	1938	112
T. Williams	Boston	1939	145
W. Dropo	Boston	1950	144
A. Rosen	Cleveland	1950	116
L. Easter	Cleveland	1950	107
F. Malzone	Boston	1957	103
F. Lynn	Boston	1975	105
J. Rice	Boston	1975	102
A. Davis	Seattle	1984	116
J. Conseco	Oakland	1986	117
W. Joyner	California	1986	100

National League

Name	Team	Year	Total
G. Wright	Pittsburgh	1924	111
D. Bissonette	Brooklyn	1928	106
P. Whitney	Philadelphia	1928	103
W. Berger	Boston	1930	119
G. Suhr	Pittsburgh	1930	107
B. Brubaker	Pittsburgh	1936	102
J. Rizzo	Pittsburgh	1938	111
F. McCormick	Cincinnati	1938	106
M. Van Robays	Pittsburgh	1940	116
B. Young	New York	1940	101
R. Jablonski	St. Louis	1953	112
J. Greengrass	Cincinnati	1953	100
M. Piazza	Los Angeles	1993	112
A. Pujols	St. Louis	2001	130
R. Zimmerman	Washington	2006	110

M. McGwire	Oakland	1987	118
H. Matsui	Yankees	2003	106
J. Abreu	Chicago	2014	107

Rookie One Hundred RBI Team

First Base	H. Trosky
Second Base	T. Lazzeri
Short Stop	G. Wright
Third Base	K. Keltner
Outfield	A. Simmons
Outfield	J. DiMaggio
Outfield	T. Williams
Catcher	M. Piazza

Rookie Team Mates With One Hundred RBI's

As noted before it has been done three times, with Cleveland doing it twice.

American League

Team	Year	Names	RBI's
Cleveland	1938	K. Keltner	113
		J. Heath	112
Cleveland	1950	L. Easter	107
		A. Rosen	116
Boston	1975	F. Lynn	105
		J. Rice	102

Rookies With Two Hundred hits

This was done only done eighteen times in the game's history. Ichiro Suzuki was the last to do it in 2001, when he set the record at two hundred forty-two. "Shoeless" Joe Jackson's name does not appear because there is a dispute whether he was a rookie in 1911. If you like you could put his name with the others. He had 233 hits for Cleveland that year.

By the way, notice that Detroit is the only team to have a pair of rookies with two hundred hits in the same year.

American League

Year	Name	Team	Hits
1927	E. Combs	New York	231
1929	D. Alexander	Detroit	215
1934	H. Trosky	Cleveland	206
1936	J. DiMaggio	New York	206
1942	J. Pesky	Boston	205
1943	D. Wakefield	Detroit	200
1953	H. Kuenn	Detroit	209
1964	T. Oliva	Minnesota	217
1987	K. Seitzer	Kansas City	207
1997	N. Garciaparra	Boston	209
2001	I. Suzuki	Seattle	242

National League

Year	Name	Team	Hits
1899	J. Williams	Pittsburgh	217
1927	L. Waner	Pittsburgh	223
1929	J. Fredricks	Brooklyn	206
1932	B. Herman	Chicago	206
1938	F. McCormick	Cincinnati	209
1964	D. Allen	Philadelphia	201

Note: Hal Trosky is the only rookie in the game's history to hit over .300 with thirty plus home runs, one hundred plus RBI's and two hundred plus hits. Joe DiMaggio in 1936 failed by one homer to duplicate Trosky's performance. In 1997, Nomar Garciaparra missed by two RBI's to place his name with Trosky.

Rookies with Thirty Homers and One Hundred RBI's

 The two categories combined dwindles down to a list of ten. Only one Hall of Famer's name is on there. Eventually, three others will be enshrined. The National only had one name, but sixty-three years later Mike Piazza emerged. Albert Pujols also arrived in 2001. Just goes to show how greatness is a rare commodity.

American League

Name	Team	Year	Home Runs	RBI
H. Trosky	Cleveland	1934	35	142
R. York	Detroit	1937	35	103
T. Williams	Boston	1939	31	145
A. Rosen	Cleveland	1950	37	116
W. Dropo	Boston	1950	34	144
J. Conseco	Oakland	1986	33	117
M. McGwire	Oakland	1987	49	118
J. Abreu	Chicago	2014	36	107

National League

W. Berger	Boston	1930	38	119
M. Piazza	Los Angeles	1993	35	112
A. Pujols	St. Louis	2001	37	130

Rookies Leading the League In Home Runs

This too is a short list with four names. Both leagues claim two names each.

American League

1950	Al Rosen	Cleveland	37
1987	Mark McGwire	Oakland	49

National League

| 1904 | Harry Lumley | Brooklyn | 9 |
| 1946 | Ralph Kiner | Pittsburgh | 23 |

Rookies Leading the League In RBI's

Only two for this category with the Boston Red Sox claiming both hitters. Ted Williams set the record for the first year men with 145. Eleven years later, Walt Dropo almost eucalypt it with 144. Ted was injured that year and had to watch Dropo make Volant try to pass the record. Dropo tied for the league lead with teammate Vern Stephens at 144. Ironically, Walt never hit the century mark again in ribbies.

American League

| 1939 | Ted Williams | Boston | 145 |
| 1950 | Walt Dropo | Boston | 144 |

National League

Never Accomplished

Rookies Leading The League In Slugging average

Again only four men did this as rookies. Fred Lynn broke the ice for yearlings in this category. Mark McGwire became the second on strength of his rookie record of forty-nine homers. Ryan Braun in what many sportswriters called the most dominant season by a rookie in Baseball History. Braun finished with a rookie slugging record of .634.

1975	Fred Lynn	Boston	.566
1987	Mark McGwire	Oakland	.585
2007	Ryan Braun	Milwaukee	.634
2014	Jose Abreu	Chicago AL	.581

Rookies Leading the League In Runs

A sparse list that has only two names. Amazingly, both men did it the same year, and both were selected over whelming as rookie of the year.

American League
| 1964 | Tony Olivia | Minnesota | 109 |
| 2012 | Mike Trout | Los Angeles | 129 |

National League
| 1964 | Dick Allen | Philadelphia | 125 |

Rookies Leading the League in Hits

This has been done nine times with eight done by American Leaguers. The one lone National Leaguer is a name from the past; Frank McCormick was up briefly in 1934 and 1937, with Cincinnati and played a handful of games. He stayed for good in 1938, which under the stipulations back then made him a rookie. McCormick was also as good a fielder as he was a hitter. He led the league three consecutive years in hits and once in RBI's. He was the mainstay of the Red's offense leading them to two pennants and award championship. He was voted MVP in 1940.

American League

1929	Dave Alexander	Detroit	215
1942	Johnny Pesky	Boston	205
1943	Dick Wakefield	Detroit	200
1953	Harvey Kuenn	Detroit	201
1964	Tony Olivia	Minnesota	217
1987	Kevin Seltzer	Kansas City	207
1997	Nomar Garciaparra	Boston	209
2001	Ichiro Suzuki	Seattle	242

National League

1938   Frank McCormick   Cincinnati   209

Rookie Pitchers with Thirty Wins In Their Rookie Year

It looks like a lot with thirty-two names, but when you take in to consideration how many have achieved it in the last fifty-one years its not so common now. It has been fifty years since the American League has had a twenty game winning rookie. The National League has had only one since 1953. All these are from the modern era (1900 on). Scanning the list you will notice in 1937, the Boston Bees had two rookies to break the twenty game mark.

American League

1901	Roscoe Miller	Detroit	23-13
1901	Roy Patterson	Chicago	20-15
1908	Ed Simmers	Detroit	24-12
1910	Russ Ford	New York	26-6
1911	Vean Gregg	Cleveland	23-7
1912	Hugh Bedient	Boston	20-9
1913	Reb Russell	Chicago	22-16
1918	Scott Perry	Philadelphia	20-19
1929	Wes Ferrell	Cleveland	21-10
1932	Monte Weaver	Washington	22-10
1945	Dave Ferriss	Boston	21-10
1948	Gene Bearden	Cleveland	20-7
1949	Alex Kellner	Philadelphia	20-12
1954	Bob Grim	New York	20-6

National League

| 1901 | Christy Mathewson | New York | 20-17 |
| 1903 | Henry Schmidt | Brooklyn | 22-13 |

1903	Jacob Weimer	Chicago	20-8
1905	Irv Young	Boston	20-21
1906	Jack Pfiester	Chicago	20-8
1908	George McQuillan	Philadelphia	23-17
1910	Leonard Cole	Chicago	20-4
1911	Grove Alexander	Philadelphia	28-13
1912	Larry Cheney	Chicago	26-10
1914	Jeff Pfeffer	Brooklyn	23-12
1937	Cliff Melton	New York	20-9
1937	Lou Fette	Boston	20-10
1937	Jim Turner	Boston	20-11
1942	Johnny Beazley	St. Louis	21-6
1944	Bill Voiselle	New York	21-16
1947	Larry Jansen	New York	21-5
1953	Harvey Haddix	St. Louis	20-9
1985	Tom Browning	Cincinnati	20-9

Rookie Pitchers Who Led The League In Victories

A very small group of three with the lone American Leaguer not being a twenty game winner.

American League
1960   C. Estrada   Baltimore   18-11

National League
1911   G. Alexander   Philadelphia   28-13
1912   L. Cheney   Chicago   26-10

Rookie Pitchers Who Led the League In ERA

Only nine have done since 1900. Officially, ERA did not become an official statistic until 1912 in the National League, and in 1913 in the American League. When true baseball researchers and historians decided to search the archives for missing information to create a complete baseball encyclopedia, they came up with the data. This led to the McMillan Encyclopedia, commonly known as the "Big Mac." Since other resource books followed such, as total baseball the figures agree almost at 100%.

American League

1909	Harry Krause	Philadelphia	1.39
1927	Willy Moore	New York	2.28
1948	Gene Bearden	Cleveland	2.43
1963	Gary Peters	Chicago	2.33
1976	Mark Fidrych	Detroit	2.34

National League

1912	Jeff Tesreau	New York	1.96
1937	Jim Turner	Boston	2.38
1951	Chet Nichols	Boston	2.88
1952	Hoyt Wilhelm	New York	2.43

Rookie Pitchers Who Led the League In Shut Outs

The count here is sixteen with the National League hogging the list with ten. Again, notice in 1937 that the same two rookies who won twenty games for the Bee's led the league in shutouts, the only time that has happened.

American League

1902	A. Joss	Cleveland	5
1949	M. Garcia	Cleveland	6
1983	M. Boddicker	Baltimore	5
2006	J. Sowers	Cleveland	2
2015	M. Montgomery	Seattle	2

National League

1911	G. Alexander	Philadelphia	7
1922	D. Vance	Brooklyn	6
1937	L. Fette	Boston	5
1937	J. Turner	Boston	5
1946	E. Blackwell	Cincinnati	6
1949	D. Newcomb	Brooklyn	5
1953	H. Haddix	St. Louis	6
1966	L. Jaster	St. Louis	5
1981	F. Valenzuela	Los Angeles	8
1995	H. Nomo	Los Angeles	3
2009	J.A. Happ	Philadelphia	2

Rookie Pitchers Leading the League in Strike Outs

This has only been done five times. The interesting fact here is that two years, both leagues were led by rookie pitchers in strikeouts.

American League

1955	H. Score	Cleveland	245
1984	M. Langston	Seattle	204

National League

1955	S. Jones	Chicago	198
1984	D. Gooden	New York	276
1995	H. Nomo	Los Angeles	236

Rookie Two Hundred Strike Out Pitchers

Again another group where the National League shows its dominance in rookie pitchers. Nine of the fifteen times was done in the National League.

American League

1910	R. Ford	New York	209
1955	H. Score	Cleveland	245
1970	B. Johnson	Kansas City	206
1984	M. Langston	Seattle	204
2007	D. Matsuzaka	Boston	201
2012	Y. Darvish	Texas	221

National League

1901	T. Hughes	Chicago	225
1901	C. Mathewson	New York	221
1911	G. Alexander	Philadelphia	227
1966	D. Sutton	Los Angeles	209
1967	G. Nolan	Cincinnati	206
1975	J. Montefusco	San Francisco	215
1984	D. Gooden	New York	276
1995	H. Nomo	Los Angeles	236

Managers Trivia

Teams who Won Consecutive Pennants with Two Different Managers

You would think that if a manager led his team to a pennant, he would be the logical choice to lead them to a repeat. This happened three times in the history of the game. After the New York Yankees won the 1960 Pennant with Casey Stengel at the helm, the Yankees right after that World Series canned the "Old Professor" as being too old. They claimed their policy was to retire anyone who reached age seventy. Casey had turned seventy at the end of July and guided the Yankees through a close race. He ended the Pennant race with a fifteen game winning streak.

The second occurrence also involved the Yankees. Ralph Houk, after winning the 1963 Pennant, was elevated to the post of General Manager. His personal choice to replace was Yogi Berra. Berra brought the Bombers home but lost in the Series to the St. Louis Cardinals. Houk fired Berra and replaced him with Johnny Keane who quit the Cardinals, who were going to fire him if he lost the Pennant.

The third case was Dick Williams quitting after two straight World Series wins. Williams could not take owner Charlie Finley's inane antics so the Oakland A's replaced him with Al Dark.

Team	Year	Manager
New York Yankees	1960	C. Stengel
New York Yankees	1961	R. Houk
New York Yankees	1963	R. Houk
New York Yankees	1964	Y. Berra
Oakland A's	1973	D. Williams
Oakland A's	1974	A. Dark

Managers Fired After Winning The Pennant

We know what happened to Casey Stengel in 1960, and Yogi Berra in 1964, but the case with Rogers Hornsby was a different turn of events. Hornsby was considered the greatest right hand hitter ever, and was the player-manager for the St. Louis Cardinals. He guided them to the World Championship in 1926. At the end of the year, he got into a hot dispute with owner Sam Breadon, "The Rajar", a highly spirited and opinionated individual. Breadon, a tightwad with a buck, could not agree on what Hornsby was worth. Breadon not only fired him but also traded him to the New York Giants for Frankie Frisch.

American League

| C. Stengel | New York Yankees | 1960 |
| Y. Berra | New York Yankees | 1964 |

National League

| R. Hornsby | St. Louis Cardinals | 1926 |

Rookie Managers Winning Pennants

Most on the list of managers are true rookie helmsmen except with the inclusion of Dallas Green and Tom Kelly. They both took over teams that were playing out the schedule. The following year, which was their first full year of managing, they were successful in leading the team to the World Championship.

American League

Clark Griffith	Chicago	1901
Hughie Jennings	Detroit	1907
Kid Gleason	Chicago	1919
Bucky Harris	Washington	1924
Joe Crown	Washington	1933
Mickey Cochrane	Detroit	1934
Ralph Houk	New York	1961
Yogi Berra	New York	1964
Dick Williams	Boston	1967
Jim Frey	Kansas City	1980
Harvey Kuenn	Milwaukee	1982*
Tom Kelly	Minnesota	1987*

National League

Pat Moran	Philadelphia	1915
Gabby Street	St. Louis	1930*
Charlie Grimm	Chicago	1932
Gabby Hartnett	Chicago	1938

Eddie Dyer	St. Louis	1946
Sparky Anderson	Cincinnati	1970
Tommy Lasorda	Los Angeles	1977
Dallas Green	Philadelphia	1980*
Bob Brenly	Arizona	2001

*Kuenn managed 1 game in 1975
*Kelly managed 23 games in 1986
*Street managed 1 game in 1929
*Green managed 30 games in 1979

Managers Who Won One Hundred Games in Their First Year

There are four to this date. Only Dick Howser did not win the Pennant but captured the American League East. Ralph Houk was the only manager to win the World Series, no great achievement since he inherited a made to order team set up by George Weiss and Casey Stengel.

Mickey Cochrane	1934	Detroit	101
Ralph Houk	1961	New York Yankees	109
Sparky Anderson	1970	Cincinnati	102
Dick Howser	1980	New York Yankees	103

Managers Who Won One Hundred or More Games in a Season Four or More Times

This category claims seven men, with Joe McCarthy and Bobby Cox leading the list with six. Only Frank Chance and Earl Weaver failed to come in first in one of their century years.

American League

Connie Mack			Earl Weaver		
1929	Philadelphia	104-46	1969	Baltimore	109-53
1930	Philadelphia	102-52	1970	Baltimore	108-54

| 1931 | Philadelphia | 107-45 | 1971 | Baltimore | 101-57 |

National League

Bill Southworth			Bobby Cox		
1942	St. Louis	106-48	1997	Atlanta	101-61
1943	St. Louis	105-49	1998	Atlanta	106-56
1944	St. Louis	105-49	1999	Atlanta	103-59

Managers Who Won Pennants in Both Leagues

A very short list of five. Ironically, two of them would face off against each other in the 1984 World Series. The winner would have the honor of being the first and to date the only one that would win a World Series in both leagues.

J. McCarthy			Y. Berra		
1929	Chicago	National League	1964	New York	American League
1932	New York	American League*	1973	New York	National League
1936	New York	American League*			
1937	New York	American League*			
1938	New York	American League*			
1939	New York	American League*			
1941	New York	American League*			
1942	New York	American League			
1943	New York	American League*			

A. Dark			D. Williams		
1962	San Francisco	National League	1967	Boston	American League
1974	Oakland	American League	1972	Oakland	American League*
			1973	Oakland	American League*
			1984	San Diego	National League

S. Anderson		
1970	Cincinnati	National League
1972	Cincinnati	National League
1975	Cincinnati	National League*

1976	Cincinnati	National League*
1984	Detroit	American League*

*World Series winners

Notice that "Sparky" Anderson is the only manager to win a World Championship in both leagues.

Managers Whose Teams Lost One Hundred or More Games Three Consecutive Years

Another short list of four names. Only two of the four were fired. Connie Mack owned the team and Casey Stengel retired mid-way the following year after breaking his hip.

American League

Connie Mack			Roy Hartsfield		
1919 Philadelphia	36-104		1977 Toronto	54-107
1920 Philadelphia	48-106		1978 Toronto	59-102
1921 Philadelphia	53-100		1979 Toronto	53-109

National League

Doc Prothro			Casey Stengel		
1939 Philadelphia	45-106		1962 New York	40-120
1940 Philadelphia	50-103		1963 New York	51-111
1941 Philadelphia	43-111		1964 New York	53-109

Manager Who's Teams Finished In Last Place
Three Or More Consecutive Years

This negative achievement was done by six men, with one doing it twice. Connie Mack is the culprit who has that distinction, but he was the owner of the team. There was no way he was going to give himself a pink slip.

American League

Connie Mack
1915 Philadelphia   43-109
1916 Philadelphia   36-117
1917 Philadelphia   55-98
1918 Philadelphia   52-76
1919 Philadelphia   36-104
1920 Philadelphia   48-106
1921 Philadelphia   53-100
1940 Philadelphia   54-100
1941 Philadelphia   64-90
1942 Philadelphia   55-99
1943 Philadelphia   49-105

Bill Carrigan
1927 Boston   51-103
1928 Boston   57-96
1929 Boston   58-96
Roy Hartfield
1977 Toronto   54-107
1978 Toronto   59-102
1979 Toronto   53-109

National League

Doc Prothro
1939 Philadelphia   45-106
1940 Philadelphia   50-103
1941 Philadelphia   43-111

Fred Haney
1953 Pittsburgh   50-104
1954 Pittsburgh   53-101
1955 Pittsburgh   60-94

Casey Stengel
1962 New York   40-120
1963 New York   51-111
1964 New York   53-109

Only Managers Who Managed Three Different Teams in a World Series

Only Bill McKechnie and Dick Williams did it. Both were successful twice.

B. McKechnie			D. Williams		
1925 Pittsburgh	National League*		1967 Boston	American League	
1928 St. Louis	National League		1972 Oakland	American League*	
1939 Cincinnati	National League		1973 Oakland	American League*	
1940 Cincinnati	National League*		1984 San Diego	National League	

*won World Series

World Series Managers Both Leagues

Only five can lay claim to that fact. Two of them faced off against each other in series. The winning manager became the only one in history to win a Series in both leagues. Who could that be? None other than "Captain Hook", "Sparky" Anderson.

	American League	National League
Joe McCarthy	New York 1932, 1936-1939, 1941-1943	Chicago 1920
Yogi Berra	New York 1964	New York 1973
Sparky Anderson	Detroit 1984	Cincinnati 1970, 1972, 1975, 1976
Dick Williams	Boston 1967	San Diego 1984
	Oakland 1972, 1973	

Managers Ejected from World Series Games

In 1907, Hughie Jennings set the precedent for a manager being ejected from a World Series game. Six others would find themselves being given the thumb over the years. The last has the distinction of being booted twice.

Year	Name	Team	Game
1907	Hughie Jennings	Detroit American League	2
1910	Frank Chance	Chicago National League	3
1935	Charlie Grimm	Chicago National League	3
1969	Earl Weaver	Baltimore American League	4
1976	Billy Martin	New York American League	4
1985	Whitey Herzog	St. Louis National League	7
1992	Bobby Cox	Atlanta National League	3
1996	Bobby Cox	Atlanta National League	6

A

B

C

Cy Young, 5, 12, 16, 20, 65, 66, 67, 68, 69, 72, 73

D

Dennis Martinez, 5
Dan Wilson, 14, 25, 33, 44, 45
Dan Wilson, **43**, **44**
Darryl Strawberry, **53**
Dave Justice, **53**
Denny McLain, **66**, **71**, **73**
Derek Jeter, **69**, **72**, **101**
Detroit Tigers, 6, 19
Dick Dietz, 25
Dick Williams, **88**, **89**, **92**, **93**
Dom DiMaggio, **47**
Don Drysdale, 25, 26

E

Enos Slaughter, **64**, **65**

F

F. Jenkins, 5, 9, 26
Frank Gustine, **31**
Frank Robinson, **65**, **66**, **70**, **71**, **72**

G

G. Perry, 5, 9, 28, 29
Gene Moore, **32**
George Mullin, 6
Greg Maddux, **73**
Guy "Doc" White, 25, 26

H

Hal Newhouser, **77**
Roy Halladay, 27, 100
Bryce Harper, 96

Harry Heilman, **32**
Hideo Nomo, 12, 20, 74

I

Ichiro Suzuki, **81**, **84**
Ivy Wingo, **43**

J

Jim Bunning, 5, 14, 25
118   106, 5
J. Maloney, 14
Jack Coombs, **61**
Joe McGinnity, 6, 27
Joe Wood,, 3
John Clarkson, 15
John Smoltz, **73**
Johnny Keane, **88**
Johnny Vandermeer, 12, 19

K

Ken Holtzman, 14
Clayton Kershaw, 21, 22, 25, 92, 93, 100
Kirk Gibson, **65**
Craig Kimbrel, 101

L

L. Aparicio, **34**, **40**, **75**
Lefty Grove, 21
Tim Lincecum, 20
Evan Longoria, 101
Lou Brock, **46**
Lou Gehrig, **72**
Louisville Colonels, 20

M

Ryan Madson, 84
Mark McGwire, 101, 107, 110, 112, 113
Matt Williams, **65**
Milt Pappas, 5

N

N. Ryan, 5, 14, 19
<u>National League</u>, 3, 4, 5, 6, 7, 8, 9, 10, 11, 12, 13, 14, 15, 16, 17, 18,
    19, 20, 27, 28, 29, 30, 31, 32, 33, 34, 35, 37, 38, 39, 40, 41, 42, 43,
    44, 45, 46, 47, 48, 49, 50, 51, 52, 53, 54, 55, 56, 57, 58, 59, 60, 61,
    62, 63, 64, 65, 66, 67, 68, 69, 70, 71, 72, 73, 74, 75, 76, 78, 79, 80,
    82, 83, 84, 85, 86, 87, 88, 89, 90, 91, 92, 93
National League., 3, 8, 35, 41, 42, 48, 69, 87
New York Giants, 3, 27, 31, 48, 88
Nolan Ryan, 12, 20

O

Orland Cepeda, **66**

P

Pete Rose, **30**, **71**
Jake Peavy, 25, 100
Albert Pujols, 89, 92, 94, 96, 101, 108, 121

R

R. Johnson, 5, 10, 31, 49, 62
Ralph Houk, **88**, **89**
Randy Johnson, 5, 20, 62, 74
Reggie Jackson, **46**, **52**, **71**
Reggie Smith, **65**
Richie Ashburn, **46**, **47**
Robert "Lefty" Grove, 23
Roger Clemens, 18, 21, 24, 73
Roger Maris, **65**, **71**